Praise for *Life Planning for You*

"Nearly all financial planners assume that their purpose is to increase your wealth. To them it seems obvious; what else could it be? Yet if someone said that the purpose of a painting is to cover a wall or that the purpose of living is to eat – we would surely disagree. Yet this is the norm in financial planning. Until George Kinder, that is. No one has done more to hammer home the true role of financial planning – to use wealth to enable us to achieve our larger life goals. This is Life Planning. In this book, Kinder makes it crystal clear – for the client, for the planner, and for the larger industry – what must be done. A cornerstone work for this new major step in financial planning."
— Charles H. Green, Founder/CEO Trusted Advisor Associates, co-author, *The Trusted Advisor*

"At last! A book that gives you step by step instructions on how to live the life of your dreams without the stress that comes with money worries. George will gently guide you to a full blazing torch - whether you light it yourself or with the help of a Financial Life Planner. He will show you how to shake off the shackles that the banks have tried to place on us all and show you how to truly attain peace of mind around money. George is a legend in the industry. We've been waiting for this book for a long time. Thank you George."
— Tina Weeks, Financial Life Planner and founder of Serenity Financial Planning

"Have you ever been inspired to get back in touch with what you wanted in and for your life? I have, when George Kinder lit my torch during the EVOKE® Life Planning process. It changed my life. This is a great book. Read it and take steps to change your relationship with your life and your money forever."
— Bruce Wilson, former Managing Director of Helm Godfrey, Director of Nucleus and former Vice President of IFP

About Kinder's *Transforming Suffering into Wisdom*

"In Suffering's Wisdom, George Kinder has written a meditation book that pulls off the impossible, being instantly accessible and at the same time extremely sophisticated, applying meditation to our most mundane moments and habitual behaviors, while on each page appealing to our highest aspirations to lead more joyous and meaningful lives. This is an exceptionally personal book, from a teacher who has truly lived his meditation practice and constantly renewed it with creativity and passion. Every page is an inspiration and a gift. Don't miss it!"
— Joel Gluck, MEd

Life Planning for You

*How to Design & Deliver
the
Life of Your Dreams*

featuring

A Comprehensive Guide to Finding
a Financial Adviser You can Trust

George Kinder

with Mary Rowland

www.lifeplanningforyou.com

The relevance of money is in moments, not in pounds, dollars or cents.
Money properly used, regardless of circumstances,
Brings us to life,
And not just to life, but to our most longed-for life.
To fulfill this heart's core yearning is our dream of freedom.
Life Planning exists to deliver that freedom to you.

Library of Congress Control Number: 2014901792
ISBN 978-0-9791743-6-0
Copyright © 2014 George D. Kinder
First Edition US

Printed in the United States of America

Serenity Point Press
business@serenitypoint.org
www.serenitypoint.org

Cover photography by George Kinder
www.georgekinderphotography.com

Cover and book design by Nadine Mazzola
www.nmazzola.com

Dedicated to

Maryellen Grady and Nadine Mazzola

Peter, Dan and Tom Kinder

and

The Life Planning community now in 25 countries

Acknowledgements

A great many people had a hand in shaping this book and to each one of you I owe a huge debt of gratitude.

First and foremost I want to thank Mary Rowland, my steadfast co-author, for her abundant insight, excellent interview and professional writing skills, and exceptional patience from our first conversation about collaboration to the final product. I couldn't have done this without her. Her months of research shaped the framework of this manuscript and her deep knowledge of consumer finance lent credibility to the structure and message of this work. To her, greatest thanks.

An extraordinary thank you as well to Chris Weetman for his fine research of UK organizations and standards and for his excellent writing in incorporating his knowledge into the book; he also spent countless hours reading, editing and standardising the spelling and grammar to the UK format. Chris is a financial Life Planner working for Otus Financial Planning (otusfp.com) in Altrincham, Cheshire. He has completed the Seven Stages and EVOKE® Life Planning courses with the Kinder Institute and has over 25 years experience in the financial world. He is both a Chartered and Certified Financial Planner^{CM}.

Many of the Registered Life Planners® consulted in writing the book contributed stories, insights and inspiration as well as the tremendous gift of their time. Whether or not your stories appear in the book, know that I wished I could have included them all. I have learned so much from your work with clients and from your skillful and inspirational application of the EVOKE® Life Planning process, and tried to convey your passion and dedication in the re-telling. My sincerest thanks to:

Mike Aitken

Dan Boyce

Stephen Brody

Anja Luesink

David Maurice

Peter Maxwell-Lyte

Steve Conley
Jeremy Deedes
Jos Drees
Phil Dyer
Michael Fairweather
Bryan Gasparro
Jay Gershman
Simonne Gnessen
Tom Greider
James Harvey
Victoria Honohan
Luella Keeley
Nicholas Lee

Chris Mellor
Alan Moran
James Norton
Dante Peters
Charles Robertson
Jeremy Squibb
Ken Sutherland
Mark Weeks
Antony Williams
Bruce Wilson
Jason Witcombe
Gary Witten

Among the Kinder Institute Trainers and RLPs® who were interviewed by Mary or myself and to those of you who contributed significantly to the stories or design of the book I am deeply grateful. Our work together as well as your work with your clients has inspired whatever wisdom is reflected in this manuscript. Thank you most for your dedication to Life Planning, now spread over many years and many countries. Your work is what has established Life Planning as the way financial firms of the future will always address finance, modeling integrity and delivering freedom into the lives of our clients:

Nigel Barker-Smith
Thom Boot
Jane Brendgen
Reed Fraasa
Peggy Frye
Joel Gluck
Ed Jacobson
Justin King
Lisa Kirchenbauer

Rosemarie McKinnon
Julian Powe
Martin Siesta
Gerard van der Made
Gabri Verbeek
Louis Vollebregt
Tina Weeks
Mary Zimmerman

Others, friends and colleagues, who engaged in conversations and shared correspondence influenced the writing of this book. I thank you all:

Sam Adams	Sheryl Garrett
Scott Bennett	Charlie Green
Danby Bloch	David Jones
Jude Boudreaux	Rick Kahler
Phil Calvert	William Kuehl
Bob Clark	Jacob Needleman
John Coughlin	Tom Neel
Roy Diliberto	Marie Swift
Lee Eisenberg	Bob Veres
Jake Engle	Richard Wagner
Harold Evensky	Mark Williamson

My heartfelt thanks to Hilary Harts, Joan Luzier, Albert Zeman and my entire Inner Listening community in Hawaii, Massachusetts, London and Holland who helped me deepen my ideas and my understanding of the roots of Life Planning. For me you have each been a source of inspiration over the years.

My gratitude to my staff who were extraordinary in their dedication. Each of you thought deeply and professionally about the message, presentation, technical and general issues around the book. Even more, you were there day after day, wrestling with the issues, refining the message, supporting and inspiring each other and myself as well as the broader community that we touch.

Jerry Cogliano for his expertise and professional advice on positioning and marketing the book. Maryellen Grady for her thoughtful readings of the book, for challenging me and suggesting improvements along the way, and for skillfully copy editing the final version. Nadine Mazzola for her keen design sense, technical abilities and expertise in laying out the book. Rae LaFont and Mary Hollinger for their social media savvy and early efforts to launch a successful marketing campaign. Most of all you have been my greatest friends in this endeavor.

Great thanks as well to each of my brothers, to Dan for his enthusiasm and excitement about the project, to Peter who has been most skillful with his vast experience in the financial world, both in the UK and the US and indeed all over the world. And I cannot thank enough my brother, Tom Kinder, who grasped the book at every level and reflected deeply about the content and purpose of the material. Many, many thanks for the countless hours you spent clarifying the message and polishing the manuscript.

My most personal and greatest gratitude is to my wife, Kathy Lubar, for endlessly encouraging and supporting me in the development of my ideas over the years, for reading and suggesting improvements over many iterations of the manuscript and for your enormous help managing all aspects of the work. Most important, thank you for your love and patience throughout this arduous effort.

My daughters, Rachel and London Kinder, have delighted me with their love and joyful spirits. I am inspired by them to leave the world a better place.

So many others contributed to this book. Many directly and some without knowing it. My apologies to the many friends and colleagues I may have overlooked who touched me in important ways and most certainly shaped my ideas.

George Kinder
Hana, Maui
January 2014

Table of Contents

Introduction

A Harris Poll recently revealed the 10 most disliked companies in America. You can probably guess the results. Six of the 10 were financial services companies, all reminders of the murky depths and shady dealings of the banking crisis and its aftermath: AIG at No. 1, Goldman Sachs at No. 2, and Bank of America, Citigroup, JP Morgan Chase, and Wells Fargo rounding out the lot.

It is easy to dislike financial services companies. We watched billion dollar bailouts handed to them, followed swiftly by billion dollar lawsuits for fraud and other criminal behavior. People all over the world lost their homes, their life savings, their retirement and their jobs in the crash that followed the financial excesses from which financial services companies greatly prospered.

Yet in this era of outrage at financial services, something radically different has been developing, something honest and inspirational, something healthy and authentic right in the midst of the world of financial advice. Small, but hopeful and even beautiful, like flowers growing in an abandoned city lot, Life Planning has begun to flourish in countries all over the world. Life Planning is a financial movement dedicated to delivering people into lives of greatest vitality, purpose and meaning – for all people, all over the world, lives supported by honest, sound and sensible financial advice. Life Planning is dedicated to supporting the client, not selling products. Most of its advisers are part of a larger movement to bring genuine fiduciary advice to clients rather than product sales to their companies' coffers. Many work with consumers of all economic circumstances, not just those with money to invest. Life Planners are dedicated to lives not products.

But I am writing about Life Planning for you, as the title says, to bring all the benefits of this movement to you regardless of whether you choose to hire a financial adviser or not.

Life Planning: Do You Life Plan Yourself or Find a Great Adviser?

This book has two purposes:

First and foremost to introduce you to Life Planning. I will show you in stories how people are being delivered into lives of freedom and I will show you how to Life Plan yourself so you can gain the same kind of freedom. I will give you the Life Planning skills and worksheets that can help you design and deliver the life of authenticity and meaning that you seek and were born to live, a life that is supported by clear and sustainable financial architecture. If you don't trust advisers, or simply want to do all financial work yourself, I will provide roadmaps and websites to help you arrive at the Life Plan that will excite you most, and to help you determine how to manage your finances to fulfill that plan.

Second, if you don't wish to Life Plan yourself, I will show you how to find a financial adviser you can trust – one whose primary mission is to deliver you into your Life Plan, your life of choice. This person would be different from most advisers you currently find in large institutions, in that they would act entirely in your interest as a fiduciary rather than in their company's interest. They would have been trained comprehensively with designations in both financial planning and Life Planning, and their fees would be completely transparent. Or better yet, they would receive fees only from you and not from any company that wants to sell you a product. In short I will show you how to find financial advisers who model integrity and whose mission is to deliver you into the freedom to live as your heart is calling you to live.

Life Planning Stories

Here are some examples of what Life Planners and their clients accomplish:

A few years ago, before the financial crisis, Martin Siesta, a Registered Life Planner® (RLP®) in New Jersey worked with a client I'll call Wilbur. Wilbur worked on Wall Street as a foreign exchange trader. His job was exhausting and stressful and he was unhappy. His unhappiness impacted his family life with both his wife and children, but he saw no way out. None of them liked the city and for years he and his wife had dreamed of running a bed and breakfast in Vermont in retirement, but it was just a dream to them, something to take their minds off the stress in their lives. Realistically it still seemed at least a decade away. They came to Martin with relatively simple insurance and pension questions, but were quite surprised when Martin seemed more interested in their life than in their money. Martin got Wilbur and his wife thinking about saving versus spending, and inspired them with his sense that the B&B might be more accessible than they thought. They cut back and tucked some money away. Within two years they bought a property in Vermont and began their transition. One year after that, Wilbur and his family moved to Vermont to take up their dream. The best part of the dream? The additional time and new experiences they were all to have together as a family.

Anja Luesink, a Registered Life Planner® in New York City worked with a young couple who wanted to make films all over the world as well as in New York. Joe had worked in independent film in his twenties, and had some great connections, but now found himself working in marketing and video production for a telecommunications company. Marilyn worked impossible hours as an interior designer, had her own office and longed to spend more time with Joe working in the film industry as well. When Anja let them know she thought their dreams were possible, it seemed to light a fire within them. In short order, they moved into Marilyn's office loft and rented out the apartment they had been living in. Joe quit his job and through his connections began getting the film work he needed to pay some bills. They sold their car, bought bikes, and became quite creative in ways to economize, saving both money and time. They were happy living a simpler, more creative and yet sustainable life aligned with their values and their creative passions.

Nicholas Lee, a Registered Life Planner® from England shared a story about his clients, Ben and Geraldine. Unmarried, they struggled financially and it was impacting their relationship. Geraldine was skeptical about working with Nicholas as a Life Planner, preferring instead to talk about practical matters such as life insurance and pensions. When directed more toward Life Planning questions she teared up, surprising both herself and Ben, by revealing she was deeply unhappy at work and was being bullied by her boss. During that first meeting Nicholas kept mostly quiet, listened and empathized while she worked out for herself what she needed to do. Much of her Life Plan involved changing her relationship to her job.

Within six months of this conversation Ben called excitedly to tell Nicholas that Geraldine, who had been on the verge of quitting, had just been asked to take a position two levels higher than her original job in the same company, nearly doubling her salary. It was around this time, Nicholas also learned, that Ben and Geraldine became engaged.

Joyce, 56, went to see a Life Planner in Philadelphia when she lost her husband and didn't know what to do with the odds and ends of financial papers he had left. As they weren't wealthy and she had never had a career or earned her own money, she was apprehensive in the meeting. For thirty years she had felt tied to her husband's life, and followed the requirements of his job. She was surprised to discover that rather than focus merely on her finances and her life in Philadelphia, the Life Planning process revealed a completely different passion, one to change her life dramatically, to live in an artists' community and to paint. The planner told her that among the odds and ends her husband had left her there was enough of a financial safety net to allow her to move out of Philadelphia and pursue her creative dreams if she cut back on expenses. Before the year was out, Joyce moved to Santa Fe, got a job three days a week in a gallery and found an apartment with a studio in it to work on her painting.

Jeremy Squibb practices Life Planning in England. Shortly after taking one of our trainings in London, he emailed me with great excitement, and with an unusual story.

"George, I've lit a Torch. I met two new clients today – twin brothers in need of guidance and pension advice. Retired, and modest in their savings, they had spoken to other advisers in the area, but came away from them, sensing they were only interested in selling products to earn a quick buck, rather than listening to their needs. Certainly their most urgent personal concern was that each of them had been diagnosed with cancer. Both were single and only had themselves and each other to consider.

Toward the end of our Life Planning discussion, which was quite poignant, it came to light that a huge underlying and unspoken desire was to travel to the other end of the country to watch Newcastle United, their favorite football team. (That's soccer for you folks in America.) It might seem odd to those of us with families, but for each of them, nothing in life mattered nearly as much as seeing as many games as possible between now and when the first of them died.

After considering both their finances and their other goals, we worked out a Life Plan that would enable them to make monthly trips to the other end of the country, flying in comfort, with good seats, and most importantly, ensuring that they had memories to share for the rest of their lives. It was amazing to see how the darkness that hung over them when they arrived lifted with the realization that they could live their dreams and follow their passions. Their concerns of mortality and financial confusion subsided, and were replaced with optimism, excitement and the anticipation of memories, which they would not only enjoy together now, but the survivor would hold for the rest of his life."

Ken Sutherland, an RLP® in North Carolina, describes a 70 year old woman, exhausted from working full-time, trapped by a high mortgage and low take-home pay, barely covering her bills. Their Life Planning work uncovered passions that she held in check because she was too tired and too poor. They included travel, photography, gardening, hiking, horseback riding, Spanish, and meeting a man; she lit up as she spoke of them and remembered how, at earlier points in her life, she was immersed in them. Most notable in her description of an ideal life was the absence of any mention of the condo where she lived. When Ken brought this to her attention, she was speechless.

Ken went on to show her how she could sell the condo, invest her equity cautiously, rent a smaller condo for less than her current monthly payment, and quit working! Her choice became very clear: she could continue her work to fund the lifestyle she had, or give up the condo to be able to retire and do the things she really wanted to do – to experience her passions sooner rather than later!

In the short term, the changes felt too frightening to do all at once, so Ken helped her establish a transition plan. Her boss would permit her to cut back to two-thirds time right away. By discontinuing her contribution to her retirement plan (already well funded), her take-home pay would not be affected. She would use her extra time and energy to begin reaching out and taking classes: Spanish, photography, gardening, etc. In the meantime, she would look into the cost of renting a condo. If those changes affirmed her desires and felt good, she would put her condo on the market, and when it sold, move to a rental and give notice to quit work entirely – or cut back to a more part-time job.

My Story

I was born with a fierce desire to live my Life Plan long before I ever knew what a Life Plan was, born with an unquenchable desire for the freedom to live the life I felt called to live – not without hard work or hardship, not without sacrifice, not without challenging recognitions and surprising transitions, but free to follow my deepest yearning wherever it led. This was clear in my youth and clear from the moment I quit graduate school. I turned down offers from top accounting firms, and instead put leaflets on cars in Cambridge, Massachusetts, advertising my services at nine dollars an hour to local residents. I would rather be poor but have freedom to pursue my passions than be well off from a job that left me too drained at the end of the day to pursue them. Throughout my life I've chosen to dedicate more time and effort to those things I most passionately want to do than to the economic tasks required to survive. Freedom (living my Life Plan) has always been most important. My passions have remained remarkably constant – to live in nature, to be wildly creative, to have a spiritual life and live a life of integrity, to sustain deep relationships, and to make a difference in the affairs of the world. When my work-life matches these passions, I work with abandon, and when it doesn't, I don't. As a consequence I have sometimes worked less than 20 hours a week, at other times more than 60, depending on what was most meaningful or most urgent at that time in my life.

Early in my adult life I began to explore the profound questions we ask ourselves (or a Life Planner asks us) in Life Planning, like how would I shape my life to fulfill my unique gifts and dreams if money were no obstacle, or how would I change my life right now if I knew I had only five years to live. As a financial adviser, I would ask those kinds of questions of my clients to bring clarity and perspective to their financial objectives, and I would ask them of myself. They became the touchstone to my freedom, to live an authentic life. I challenged myself with them several times a year. Often my responses were quite similar from year to year, but at times they revealed something new, a passion to spend much of my life doing something I had never imagined before, like living in Hawaii part of each year. Quite quickly I would pursue that passion, finding a way, for instance, to work in Hawaii, as much as in Massachusetts where I lived, in order to make it affordable. Later, I found myself surprised again with a passion to spend time in the city of London, and I now spend several months a year there, joined by my wife and children for much of it.

None of these transitions were easy, certainly not financially, but I learned very early that to block these passions was to stifle something authentic, even urgent, inside. And whenever I pursued my passions I found new and tremendous vitality in my life both to accomplish these dreams and for all my other pursuits. For instance, now, passionately engaged with a mission to change the world of money, I am delighted to be connected with the heart of the world of finance in London, while at home in Massachusetts I spend most of my days in a writer's cabin on my property, nestled in trees and bushes and surrounded by lake water. Or as another example, this is my third book on money, each refining a vision of how to deliver freedom into peoples' lives, but I've also written a book on meditative practice, *Transforming Suffering into Wisdom* (2010) and a book of poetry and photography, *A Song for Hana* (2007). That book was written to help stop threats of development along a piece of sacred Hawaiian coastline contiguous to property Oprah owns in the remote, native Hawaiian community of Hana, Maui where I live with my family part of each year.

What if we all lived our most inspired life? Our most meaningful life? What if every day we challenged ourselves to live into our dreams, to bring into being the life of greatest meaning to ourselves and those around us? What a difference that would make! For us and for the world.

Life Planning does this for everyone who opens to its transformative power. It brings passion, vitality, energy, accomplishment and inspiration into our lives, because it frees us from the clouds that have obscured our paths and blocked our promise. Time and again Life Planners have seen such transformations take place in their clients. Parents heal wounds with children and children with parents, spouses with each other. People claim a new and vital place in their communities, create one-of-a-kind businesses, challenge authorities to do the right thing, or do something significant for their environment. They choose to live with greater integrity, kindness or spiritual practice in their lives. They step out into the world of acting in independent films, or writing the memoir they have both feared and longed to reveal, or playing jazz in clubs in their neighborhoods or with their children at home. People transform their lives in ways large or small, moving always in the direction of the calling they find in their heart's core.

Imagine how the burdens and costs of society could be eased and new ventures created if we each were to live in this way. As we gain greater freedom to live our passions or our dreams, we add vitality and vigor to the economy and to our communities at the same time.

A more virtuous, entrepreneurial society filled with invention and creativity would grow out of a different societal relationship with money. Life Planning brings a more appropriate and clearer understanding of money's place in society through a full integration of our money life with who we each long to be.

I hope that you will join consumers and financial advisers all over the world who are part of this movement. In it we transform our lives, putting our financial houses in order by putting the meaning in life first. What's most surprising about this revolution, coming out of the banking crisis as it does, is that the major force globally behind it is springing up within the financial planning community, in a group of financial advisers that call themselves Life Planners.

It was my work amongst financial advisers that led me to ask Mary Rowland to join me in the writing of *Life Planning for You*. Mary is one of the finest financial journalists I know. I began to follow her work many years ago when she was personal finance columnist (for nearly a decade) with the *Sunday New York Times*. I saw her work as well in other national consumer publications. I followed her even more closely when she shifted her primary focus to financial planners and became well known for her own books on personal finance and financial advice.

Mary knows as much about personal finance as anyone I know. She has also taken all the Life Planning coursework to become a Registered Life Planner®, and has modeled living through challenging experiences into more of her own ideal life.

Both Mary and I have been in finance for over 30 years, Mary as a journalist, myself primarily as an adviser and Life Planner. We have spoken at major conventions and before audiences around the world, appeared on radio and television programs, and have written and been written about in virtually all the major news and financial periodicals in America and in many international publications as well. We have both won awards for our work and have consistently stood up for what we feel would make the world of personal financial advice more full of service, integrity and accuracy, more client-centered.

I want to thank Mary publicly for all she has done to improve the world of finance, including her invaluable help to me in the writing of this book.

Since the publication of my first book *The Seven Stages of Money Maturity* (1999) (which has been translated into German, Japanese, Korean and Dutch), I have established a global Life Planning training company, the Kinder Institute of Life Planning, training advisers on six continents. This is my life's work. Currently we list on our website nearly 2000 advisers from 25 countries who have taken our 2-Day Seven Stages workshops and an elite group of over 300 advisers who have taken a full slate of our programs and become Registered Life Planners®. This book has grown directly out of the many years of experience of those people and the evolution of the movement they have built.

The Transformation of Financial Services

Daily, whether in the news or in our lives, each of us encounters a money world that is complex and disappointing. Rarely is it known for the integrity needed to fulfill its greatest promise, which is to bring genuine freedom to all people to fulfill their callings and dreams. But I believe it can and is meant to deliver with integrity, freedom to people from all walks of life all over the world, and could do so soon. In order to do this we need a transformation of financial services. We need a trusting and inspired environment to replace the old era, the century of sales we have lived through. In particular we need structures, processes, people and brands that consumers can trust. The basis of a new world of finance must be the practice of putting the lives of people ahead of money and its products. This is the fundamental principle of Life Planning.

Here we are, going through another recession, another banking crisis, and the government is thinking the same old tired way: "Let's tweak the financial structures and then goose the economy with credit," an approach that has historically led to inflation and cycles upon cycles of boom and bust. What if we tried something different? What if instead we inspired people to live their lives to the fullest, to their greatest potential? How much untapped energy, vitality and efficiency might be released? This is what Life Planning does.

We are at an extraordinary moment in history. Although our large institutions have continued to fail us, we in the financial world now how to deliver advice with integrity and free of conflicts of interest. We know how to deliver inspiring financial advice efficiently and effectively to working class and middle income consumers as well as to the more affluent. We know how to tie financial advice to the most profound and urgent dreams of our clients so that their potential may be fulfilled. We know how to advise the consumer in simple but elegant and powerful investment methodologies that are not secret covers for high trading costs, high commissions, high risk and ultimately low returns. We know how to give comprehensive and holistic financial advice. With all of these great benefits, why are consumers not delighted with the financial industry? Because they can't find the companies that are honest, inspirational and wise. What they see instead are the same old tired companies, called out for fraud or billion dollar fines in the daily news, more dedicated to their profits and paychecks and to scrambling from the authorities than to their customers' best interests.

This book will show you how to find this new kind of adviser. I believe we are on the edge of a revolution in financial advice, when such advisers will become a name brand, increasingly easy to find, accessible to all. I'm reminded of a time nearly 20 years ago when (in America) our experience with coffee suddenly changed. For decades we used to struggle to find a good cup of coffee. It was awful! I know some scoff at Starbucks, or have other preferences. But as Starbucks suddenly appeared on street corners everywhere, branded, it became obvious how easy it was to get a great cup of coffee. The world changed.

Today, most people know where they can find a great cup of coffee, but still very few people know where to get great financial advice. This is a tragedy but also an opportunity of historic proportions. Easy to find and readily available financial advice that places the interests of the client first and their life dreams at the center of the financial plan is what clients want. The businesses that brand and deliver it will be to the world of finance what Starbucks has been to the world of coffee.

That's where the real fraud exists. As you will see in this book, there is great financial advice available now all over the world. But if great advice already exists, why have the large corporations been so laggard in delivering it and what has the government been doing to help the consumer identify it and find it? You'll find that out in the last chapter of this book, along with an inspiring vision of the transformations possible in a financial system, dedicated to delivering freedom into peoples' lives and modeling integrity in all things.

Life Planning puts our passion to work. It takes our deepest longings and it empowers us to realize them. Even when they seem impossible, it challenges us to find a way, and we nearly always do.

This book will show you how to do this, how to marry meaning and money in your life, by showing you how thousands of people are doing it either for themselves or with advisers. I will share some of their stories with you, and you will see what I mean when I say that.

Life Planning delivers freedom. It all starts with you and your dreams.

EVOKE®:
Living Your Life of Freedom

Each of us is born with a special gift, with what William Blake calls our poetic genius, with unique potential that is ours alone. Life Planning releases it from whatever holds us back. For too long, too many of us have led lives of diminished vitality but we are called each of us to come alive to our passionate purpose. This book is a call to discover our dreams, and to bring them alive by reorganizing our relationship to money in order to support our life of greatest value and meaning.

Ethan and Sarah seemed the picture of health, success and happiness. They'd owned a beautiful brownstone in Brooklyn Heights for 15 years, a time when it appreciated considerably. Both were doctors. Ethan had an impressive career at Columbia Presbyterian, a teaching hospital in New York, where he taught and managed a private practice. Sarah was involved with the community and the schools. They had three talented adolescent and teenage daughters, and an active community and religious life.

I had met them earlier that year when Sarah asked me to give a speech, in Chicago, to a physician's conference on wellness. I talked about how to develop a healthy relationship with money. In my keynote, I had talked about the power of Life Planning, and Ethan sat in, as well, on a small workshop I gave that afternoon.

A few days later, Sarah called from New York to set up an appointment. When Ethan and Sarah walked into my office in Boston, I could tell something was wrong.

Sarah seemed alert and at ease. She said she was there to support Ethan, who looked troubled. As we spoke it became clear that Sarah, who had let go of her practice as an oncologist in order to be more available for their children, was quite happy with her life. She remained connected with her medical community by taking leadership in the area of wellness and medicine while living a rich and fulfilling family life.

Ethan, on the other hand, wanted something different from his life. He wanted to be of greater service to his community. And through our conversation it became clear that he wanted to become a rabbi. He was an excellent physician, well respected by his peers and loved by his patients, but he was tired of the work, tired of the hours, the business compromises, and he wanted to live a richer life. I found him despondent in that first meeting, and as we talked, I could see why. He believed that the life of greater service, to which he felt called, was 10-15 years away — probably, realistically, 15. I watched him speak with some lightness of being and passion around his vision of being a rabbi, only to see his whole body and demeanor sink with each realization that it would take 15 years to complete the education of his three children and his own training before he could make his dream real. More often than not in our meeting, perhaps because of this pain, he preferred to limit his "dream," and he simply talked about his wish to have more sense of balance in his work, and more work-life balance in general.

I felt sad to see him this way. He was one of the more remarkable young men I have met. His external accomplishments were clear enough, but he also had an extraordinarily loving relationship with his wife (one of the most relaxed and natural marriages I'd encountered in my office), as well as with his children. Yet I could also see in the infrequent passion in his eyes that he had real vision in his bones and leadership in his blood. In those moments he was truly charismatic as he spoke from his passion, and even in his more somber moments, he was so clear and honest with his feelings that I was moved in my own. He was a splendid communicator, deep in his understandings, and had the *markings of a great teacher. All that said, he could not see that freedom to live as he felt called to do could begin to emerge much sooner. He had clearly come to the right place, I thought.*

At the end of that first meeting, Ethan seemed more hopeful, and Sarah quite happy. I got the impression that Ethan rarely spoke of his secret dreams to others, but felt so comfortable with our relationship that he could unburden himself, and that he felt a burst of freedom when he was able to talk about them. Both he and Sarah were clearly looking forward to the second meeting, but I could also see in Ethan lingering doubt and discouragement as he thought of the money and the time that would be required before he was able to immerse himself fully in what he thought he was meant to do. I simply said, when I saw this, "I think we can make something happen here, Ethan, something much closer to your dream than where you are right now." His posture straightened, his spirit seemed to lift, and there was light as well as moisture in his eyes.

EVOKE® is the name of the five-phase Life Planning process that I developed over years of working with clients like Ethan and Sarah. It is designed to deliver each person to their life's purpose, their dream of freedom, the path of passion or compassion that brings them alive. In this process, there is a complete integration of a client's vision with their finances. Their finances are brought into the service of the vision. By the testimony of hundreds of advisers and thousands of clients, it works. In this book I hope to accomplish two things:

1. I will show you how to EVOKE® your own life of freedom, using the five-step process.

2. I will also show you how EVOKE® would work if you were working with an accomplished Registered Life Planner®, and some of the advantages of working with one.

Before I return to the story of Ethan and Sarah, I think it would be useful to describe the five phases of EVOKE®, so that you can see how they worked for them and could work for you.

EVOKE® is an acronym. Each of its letters stands for a word, and each of the words describes a phase of inquiry or action or both. Here it is in just those words with a sentence describing how a Life Planner would lead you through each phase:

E for Exploration: The getting-to-know-you phase with open-ended questions and wide-open exploration.

V for Vision: The inspirational meeting where our Torches are lit, and we find ourselves on fire to accomplish our life's purpose.

O for Obstacles: The meeting where we take on all the challenges and obstacles to our dreams, and resolve them methodically but with energy and vitality, one by one.

K for Knowledge: Where we outline and write down the Life Plan, step by step, that will accomplish our dreams, including a financial strategy to accomplish the plan.

E for Execution: Where we take action on each of the steps outlined in our plan until they are all accomplished, and we are living our life of purpose.

The first meeting with Ethan and Sarah was the Exploration meeting. In it, we got to know each other pretty well. My role as an adviser was to find ways to help them feel at ease and even excited to tell me everything that could possibly be on their minds toward the purpose of a financial Life Plan, through open-ended questions, empathy and active listening. The end result is nearly always significant trust in the process and in each other. A good dose of curiosity and interest on my part helps as well, while holding to my own passionate purpose of bringing every client, if not every person, to the life they most want to lead.

If you were doing Exploration for yourself, without the aid of a financial adviser, you would be asking yourself to reflect and write down (or record) everything you can think of, financial or not, that you would like to accomplish or discuss, as if you were entering a genuinely empathic and interested Life Planner's office – the office of someone you might think of as a mentor. At the end of your own first meeting, it is likely you would feel a growing confidence, intermingling both comfort and excitement, that you were beginning the great adventure of your life.

In my second meeting (the Vision meeting) with Ethan and Sarah, I reviewed a number of goal exercises that they had completed in preparation for the meeting. We spent time on each of their dreams and passions. I was eager to learn about them all. They painted a picture of an already rich life that was poised to grow in richness as they matured. Still, I watched and gave encouragement as Ethan's despondency would return, overlapping, wave upon wave, with his dreams.

With each collapse into the "realization" that it would take 15 years to truly get to the life that he longed so passionately to live right now, I brought him back to the dreams of his goal exercises and appreciated how rich and beautiful and necessary his responses were to his living a flourishing life. I kept sprinkling in, as well, how possible I thought they all were, and as our conversation deepened, I could sense that in moments now and then, he began to believe me.

Toward the end of the meeting, when it was clear that we had covered everything essential, I paused, gathering my thoughts, and asked him the following question: "If, as a consequence of our work together, I (or we) were able to deliver to you immediately part-time work as a physician, so that you could deepen and more rapidly move forward with your rabbinical studies and within two years you were to realize this life of service you dream of, in fact you're a rabbi, serving your community in Brooklyn, your family strong and happy, and proud and delighted with the choice that you have made, how would that be?"

Ethan gulped, eyes wide open, and said immediately, "Well, there are some practical obstacles to that realization, but if you were able to deliver that to me, wow! That would be fantastic. That would be exactly what I want! I can't believe it. It would be incredible!" He glanced quickly at his wife who was smiling with all her love, and then back at me. "But you've hardly looked at our financials, and there is a required time frame to becoming a rabbi that would likely take longer than you imagine."

"Put the obstacles to the side for now, if you would, Ethan. I've looked at your financials well enough to have some confidence that I'm not too far out of the ballpark, and we'll look at the rabbinical requirements shortly, but for now what I'd like you to do is live into the dream. How it would be."

"Well, that would really be amazing," he said. "What do we do next?"

I asked him to go home and live into the dream for the next couple of weeks, to trust me around the financials, that we would work something out, and for him to begin to imagine as fully as he could what the new life would actually look like. I asked if he could come back in two weeks with a painted picture for me, and as he came up with objections or difficulties in the picture, if he would put them to one side, even write them down, but keep his eyes on the prize, and keep living into the possibility of the dream. In the next meeting, I promised, we would address all the obstacles – but it would only work if he let the dream itself become vivid, visionary, and palpable to him.

My second book, describing the EVOKE® process for financial advisers, is called *Lighting the Torch* (2006). Lighting the Torch is what happens in the Vision meeting, where the excitement becomes so palpable, and you realize that you've added a whole new level of energy and vitality into a person's life – a vitality that with your steady but gentle support, launches your client into the life they have been meant to live. It is an extraordinary moment, an extraordinary experience.

If your passion is to do this for yourself, I will guide you in the coming chapters through the exercises to identify your Torch, and the steps required to light it, so that you, too, are moving forward, impelled toward the vision of life that will bring you most meaning and most vigor.

If the Vision meeting is the moment of launch, by the end of the Obstacles meeting every imaginable system is working to make the journey successful.

When Ethan and Sarah came in to the third meeting, there was an energy in the room that I had not experienced with them before. It was as if Ethan had reclaimed his identity, reclaimed his sense of purpose. Ethan was workmanlike, with charts and graphs and spreadsheets. He still had his doubts, and there were definite moments of despair in the meeting, but he had claimed the vision as his own, and he was willing to suspend his doubt just enough to get to work genuinely on solving the problems that stood in its way – even where they rose like some enormous mountain surrounded by clouds, seemingly insurmountable in his path. For the first time, it seemed to me, he was not looking at me with some faint hope that I might be the genie who would let him out of his bottle, but rather as if we were partners, climbing a mountain together. It was exciting and it was fun.

The obstacles came fast and furiously. He had to do rabbinical studies first and the time-frame and prerequisites would keep him from meeting the two-year goal. He had inadequate time to do the study, and inadequate financial resources to take the time off to study. All of his savings were tied up in retirement vehicles with significant penalties for withdrawing any money, if any withdrawal was allowed at all. He must support his children (and his own training) for another 15 years to get through high school, college and perhaps some graduate school. His medical group discouraged part-time work by assigning fixed costs to each doctor equally; a doctor needed to work half the week just to cover the overhead before making any profit. Whew! You can see how easy it would be to fall into despondency with all this. Although we might not be as fortunate financially as a doctor, we all have our own enormous list of seemingly impossible obstacles to living into our dreams. Yet they are just as paltry and sad excuses for not living a fulfilled life as Ethan's were.

Here's what we did. You will see that this meeting often overlaps with the fourth meeting, the Knowledge meeting, which outlines our Life Plan and our financial plan and the actions we must take. In fact, my Obstacles session (which usually takes one meeting) took a few with Ethan and quite naturally overlapped with the financial plan we were putting together.

I asked Ethan to plot out the quickest route possible for his rabbinical studies. Also, to identify the stages he might go through and identify the degree of satisfaction he might achieve in each stage. I asked him as well to research the salary he might expect to earn as a rabbi. It turned out that he would be enormously happy, and feel that he had arrived at his dream, by reducing his physician's hours 40%, dedicating the rest of the time to study and apprentice service. There was a part of him that loved his medical work, and wanted to go slowly in leaving it. After two years, he felt he would be able to increase the amount of time in rabbinical service, and reduce his doctor's practice by perhaps another day. After four to five years, he felt he would be in a position to let go of his doctor's practice entirely and to become a rabbi with an average salary that surprised him – on the upside! So, this was the ideal, the dream that he could begin to live right away, and no other dream was larger than this. But how to deal with the financial obstacles?

The first thing I suggested was to immediately stop funding his retirement plan, which was keeping his money tied up so that he couldn't really get at it for years. The retirement plan had been created by a great technician, a man and a firm renowned for top-notch financial planning. Yet they still did a terrible job for this client. The plan itself was an awfully good vehicle, and would save oodles in taxes (I can just see the adviser chortling), but totally inappropriate for anyone who might step off the doctor path and seek to live a different kind of life. The planner had asked lots of questions, mostly by questionnaire, but never really took time to get to know Ethan, never listened or provided the venue for Ethan to speak deeply and from his heart. Ethan never thought it appropriate, or felt safe enough, to talk about the things he cared for most deeply. After all, he felt so guilty about seeing his life, one admired by most people in the world, as inadequate, so he kept quiet and the planner locked his assets up in vehicles he couldn't get out of for years, and locked Ethan's dreams up in clouds of confusion and despair.

If he stopped funding the retirement program going forward, he would have additional cash flow right now to help fund his dream. The next thing Ethan did was to negotiate a different kind of deal on the overhead of his physician practice. Why should someone working part-time pay the same level of overhead as someone working full-time? Those who favored the status quo, and it was a solid majority, argued that overhead is a fixed cost. Each doctor had his own office, and so should pay an equal amount to overhead. But Ethan countered that he would be happy to share an office, and that part-timers were not contributing as much to the cost of overhead because they simply were not in the office that much and therefore should not pay a full share of the expenses. Others who were troubled by the lack of balance between work and life joined Ethan's argument. Ethan was enormously respected and greatly liked in the office, which made the negotiations easier, and in the end he won the day, saving more money for current needs by reducing his overhead expenses.

For his children's education, he appealed to his father, who was retired and elderly, and was confident he would not outlast his assets, to dedicate some to the children's education now, whether in trust or covering actual costs.

We talked with Sarah about the possibility of increasing her salaried work level, and although she was enormously supportive of what we were doing, it really didn't fit into her Life Plan to add more than a few hours a week of work to her life. We crafted something for her where she did no additional hours, but got better paid for the things that she did do. We also factored in her desire to *return to the workplace in a more substantial part-time capacity as her children left the home.*

So, what with a rabbi's salary, part-time employment for Ethan in the meantime, more funds from his wife's efforts, some help from Dad, redesigning his retirement funding, and negotiating a lowering of his physician's overhead cost, we had nearly what he needed to accomplish his dream. Looking out over the rest of his life, it was only this next five-year period that we could not quite fund. For a moment we were stumped, and I could see the despondency arising again in Ethan's face. We had diminished the 15 years to probably five to ten. Good work, but not enough to keep the Torch burning brightly.

I asked him about the home they all lived in. A beautiful brownstone in one of the most desirable neighborhoods for professionals who want to raise children at the same time they work in Manhattan. He could not afford such a home on a rabbi's salary, and I asked him and Sarah if they were willing to sell it and move into more economical surroundings if it meant the realization of this dream. They took one look at each other and then exclaimed in unison, "Absolutely!" And then there was another pause of reflection. They both looked down, and after a bit, Ethan looked at me with a touch of sorrow in his eyes, and a hint of the love that lay underneath it, and said: "But there is one thing. The house means a lot to my children. It really is the place the whole neighborhood congregates, all their friends. I couldn't possibly sell it while it means so much to them." There was a lump in my throat at the possibility that all of our work might be for naught, and a gentle smile on my face as I felt a surge of appreciation. What wonderful parents these two were, what wonderful surrogate parents for their daughters' friends, how much they cared not only for their family but for making community happen. I sat there, just for a minute, in awe. I felt moisture in my eyes.

"I could never do it to them," he said. "I could never be that kind of dad." I nodded empathically, pausing again. And then I asked Ethan a question. "Ethan, can we think for a moment about the kind of dad you want to be for them? I mean, I understand what you're saying, but let's flash 15 years forward, assuming that your worst case scenario were to come true. Which would you rather model for your kids, and which would they rather say? 'My dad slaved away for 15 years, working long hours and sacrificing his calling to be a rabbi — what he really wanted to do — just so I could live in the house of my dreams?'

or would you rather have them say, and learn from your model: 'My dad had the courage, in the prime of his career as a doctor, to step out to a deeper calling, something that he longed for, something with the greatest integrity for him, even at the sacrifice of economic well-being. I am so proud of him, and all the people he has helped.'"

A bit of a sheepish grin came across his face. "You need to go home and ask them," I suggested. "Call a family meeting." And here I learned something from him. "No, you've got it wrong, George. A family meeting won't do at all. I need to talk with each of the children individually." And that's what he did.

Two weeks later he came in with some bad news and some good news. Two of the daughters, upon hearing of his proposed career change, and the possible sale of the house, simply said "Cool, Dad! Go for it!" But one of the daughters objected. She was most attached to the house, and to her community. The change would be very upsetting to her. Once again Ethan felt the impossibility of his dream intermingling with his deep love of his child. But later, he asked her another crucial question: "Would it be alright if we sold the house after you left for college," and she responded warmly, "I think that would be fine, Daddy, but could we try not to move too far away?"

Her response was key. We needed the equity from the house. We could get at it temporarily by refinancing the house. The house could then be sold off in five years as they moved to a less expensive home. There were many of them in Brooklyn Heights and in lovely parts of Brooklyn like Park Slope. The spreadsheets worked. Ethan was launched. Execution was a dream.

As you hear Ethan's story you might be struck by the differences in my work from other financial advisers you've encountered. This is a new world we are talking about, a new breed of advisers we'll introduce to you later in the book. Remember, Life Planners aren't selling appliances! Or even financial products. Here, we first bring people to the vision of the world in which they are meant to flourish. And then we make sure, to the very best of our human ability, that the financial underpinnings of that world are secure.

Without my genuine care and attention, Ethan might not have stepped into his dream. Without my knowing thoroughly and completely where he wanted to go, it is likely I would have mismanaged his financial situation, so that it didn't serve him, or even worse, so that it best served me, not him, and put him farther away from his goal. This was precisely what his prior "great" financial planner had done, by not taking the time, not giving Ethan every opportunity to reveal who he really was, not listening or using skills of thoughtful inquiry.

We have been conditioned to think that a financial adviser's office is all about money. This is a tragic mistake. Human lives are at stake. Ethan's life was at stake. Financial planning is not about money. The human life comes first. Let's find out for ourselves, as we go through the book, what the life is that is meant to be lived. Then, and only then, can we apply the financial architecture to make it happen.

Our lives run deep. If our conversation with a financial adviser can't run as deep as our own lives, we are in the dangerous situation that Ethan was in, of not living into his dream, of putting off his dream and living a despondent life for another 15 years, and very likely forever. Without nurture, dreams can simply die.

Even those who have nothing, have dreams come alive in Life Planning

The dreams that we discover in Life Planning are critical to our vitality and to a fulfilled life, even if we have nothing at all. For Gabri Verbeek, it was a couple of Life Planning workshops that changed his life in the Netherlands.

The owner of a small business with 17 employees, Gabri was already a financial planner, primarily selling products, when he took a Life Planning workshop one summer. While his life seemed charmed with a happy family and a good business, something wasn't right. His exposure to the limitless possibilities of Life Planning set him on fire. When he returned home, a colleague said: "Something's changed you."

Indeed. After the workshop, Gabri decided to sell his company and do something with Life Planning instead. He had booked a follow-up 5-Day training in London in 2008 when, in the banking crisis, his company went bankrupt. Gabri lost everything. Suddenly on shaky grounds, Gabri decided to cancel his attendance at the training. With financial concerns mounting, he was worried his wife would be furious at the expense. But when he talked with her, he discovered that she knew better: "I'd divorce you if you didn't go," she said to him. "This is what you need!"

"For three weeks after the bankruptcy, I was all mixed up," Gabri says. "All the security I thought I had in life was gone. I thank heaven for Carla and my kids. Little did they know, my body and mind were boiling like soup."

But Gabri completely changed in those five days. "On day three, I got my insight moment," he says. "I was sitting there and I could hardly speak, I had so much feeling in me. I'd built my financial company for 23 years and what I realized for the first time was that it was all about the feelings – that was what was missing in my old business. For me, it was like finding a big leak. It was about finding authenticity." He had thought that he already knew everything he needed to know about financial planning. And now he had tapped into his feelings about money. A potent combination! When he went home, his wife said: "You've got another face." Gabri says he realized that what he wanted to do was to build a business doing Life Planning for individuals that was a model of integrity, without selling a single product. And in the years that followed he has become a model for others in Holland and the UK to do just that. Through the years of struggle and poverty that followed, Gabri realized that the twin dreams of his Life Plan could never be taken from him: to have a great family and to live in integrity. Pursuing with passion his newfound dream made him strong and brought joy to his family.

Whatever our circumstances, Life Planning identifies our dream, builds it into a vision, and then gives us the vitality and financial knowledge to bring it into reality.

As we explore EVOKE® in more depth, we will first dedicate ourselves to understanding and discovering what the things are that we hold most dear, what are our passionate purposes. We will then look at how to reconfigure our lives, easily and simply, by keeping our eyes on the prize, to overcome creatively the obstacles that present themselves and to put the financial architecture together and take the practical actions to deliver that life to ourselves in the shortest possible time frame, for nearly all of us starting right away! We will also look at how financial Life Planners can streamline the process for many of us, but our primary focus will be on how we might do it all ourselves. We will hold off on a comprehensive description of how to find a great adviser until the final chapter of the book. As in a true Life Planner's office, your life comes first.

*Exploration - E*VOKE®
The Conversation of a Lifetime

We are alive at the dawning of a whole new way of addressing money. Fundamentally, it's not about the numbers. In Life Planning we have conversations that are passionate, humane, challenging, and rich with engagement; ones that free us to live into the best of our being, our brilliance, our great hearts. The Exploration meeting, the first phase of EVOKE®, is where it all begins. It can start quietly, awkwardly. It can start with emotion or a strict sense of financial purpose, but as it deepens it will become filled with authenticity if it is truly Life Planning.

Exploration is where trust is established, which is saying a lot in the world of money. It is where we are given permission to bring everything in our life, everything we have ever dreamed of into the conversation. One of the things I've learned in my nearly 40-year financial career is that there is nothing so tender nor so intimate that money doesn't impact it. So the first conversation in a Life Planning engagement whether with ourselves or with a planner, is both open and engaged. With a planner it could take as little as ten minutes or as long as an hour and a half. With ourselves it is outside of time.

There are no artificial boundaries and no agendas as this is meant to be an exploration of everything that means something to us. It's all on the table, practical concerns as well as personal. If we want to deliver a new or transformed life, this conversation, whether with ourselves or with an adviser, must occupy the largest possible psychic space, and be conducted in a framework of trust, appreciation, optimism, kindness and respect. Cynicism, skepticism and doubt are checked at the door. If we censor what we want, whether it's a revitalized relationship with our family, a sensible tax and saving program, or our lowest possible handicap at golf, our Life Plan will be incomplete and full of hidden obstacles and subterfuges. Its accomplishment will be in jeopardy. If we are married, without this kind of openness and willingness to partner around the purposes of our life, our marriage may be in trouble as well.

The conversation that we have with ourselves as we begin Exploration is rich with meaning. It puts what's most important in our lives first. In my early days of Life Planning clients would often end our first meeting by saying, "This was one of the best conversations I've ever had." And then they would say, "How come my broker never did this with me?" This was back in the days when brokers dominated the financial advice business in America, and "advice" was really about buying stocks and insurance, about products and sales. Since I was just beginning in the field I didn't realize how different Life Planning was from traditional financial "advice," but it was certainly reassuring and even exciting to realize I was, even as a rookie, doing something well. As I grew in my practice and began sharing what I did with other advisers at the top of the financial profession, most were intrigued. They recognized something different was happening and that it was good. Others among the leadership, folks we all respected would say, "I know you like to think George Kinder's work is something special but really it's not – it's just financial planning – done right." I'd like to think both camps were right. Life Planning is special. And it's just financial planning done right – done the way it should be done, discovering first and foremost how a client really wants to live their life – and then delivering it. A Life Planner becomes a genuine partner, a facilitator, in our life's construction.

Surprised by Life Planning

Alan Moran, in England, was a financial planner before he became a Registered Life Planner®. "Bill and Tracey were the last couple I would have expected to be interested in Life Planning," Alan remembers. Tracey, 55, rarely came to their quarterly check-ups and when she did, she usually just sat there and stifled a yawn. Bill, 63, made sure the meetings were run on a dime, all facts and figures. But on one occasion Bill asked why they had never been invited to work out a Life Plan. "I talked with one of your other clients and he said his real life began after working with you!" Bill had said.

Alan set up a meeting in two weeks time. When Bill and Tracey arrived for the Exploration session, Alan felt apprehensive. Bill always dominated the conversations and made all the financial decisions. Tracey seemed indifferent and Alan felt he didn't really know her.

Alan started with Tracey. It was awkward at first. Now it was Tracey who just wanted to talk figures. And then she said, "Why can't Bill stop working? I'd like to spend more time with him." As Alan gave her his full attention, sides of Tracey poured forth that Bill hadn't heard in years and that Tracey hadn't fully articulated even to herself: her childhood summers on Vinal Haven, an island off the coast of Maine, their honeymoon in the Falkland Islands, her desire to live more connected with nature and to write a memoir. "I'm afraid Bill will work till he drops," she said. "I dreamed of a life together. And now, thirty years later, I wonder if it will ever happen."

Bill was flabbergasted. He found himself falling in love again with the memories of their island adventures and with Tracey. "I'm afraid to quit working," he said. "I worry that we won't have enough money. Tracey is eight years younger. I want her to be comfortable for the rest of her life."

Then looking directly at his wife he confessed, "I don't want to work so much. I'd love to go back to those islands with you. I can still remember the sky on the Falklands, so large and blue and the ring of clouds hugging the horizon that looked like a white necklace on the sky."

"Alan, can we do something about this?"

"Absolutely," Alan replied. "I've just been waiting for you to ask."

As they left, Tracey gave Alan a hug and whispered in his ear, "That was the best conversation we've had in 33 years."

Rather than probing or directing with his comments or questions, Alan had mostly been quiet. He was really tuned into Tracey's state of mind. His questions, when he asked them, were open ended to make sure Tracey felt free to roam and that everything important got on the table for discussion. The results speak for themselves. Achieving this level of meaning and significance in the first meeting is usually a sign that the couple will in fact accomplish their Life Plan. They are already emotionally engaged and energized in the process of making it happen.

The best conversation in 33 years and yet how different this was from a "normal" conversation, even one which we think of as delightful. One might even wonder if this was a conversation. Alan hardly said a thing, but his every word and gesture expressed empathy, interest or appreciation. Quite a contrast to when we meet someone at a party or an event and instantaneously feel a connection, an energy, with shared interests, attitudes or passions. We find ourselves so excited when they mention a favorite vacation spot because we have just been there ourselves, and we dive in. We interrupt with how we walked the stony shores, who we met, where we got our supplies, the photography we did there. And then our new friend, hardly letting us finish a sentence, leaps in themselves with a question about did we use a Canon or a Nikon, and have we seen the newest long lens or ever used Lightroom, so much easier than Photoshop, at least so their daughter tells them, and then the conversation becomes all about daughters. It's a wonderful dance we do, full of excitement, fun and delight, but not *the best conversation in 33 years.*

In a financial adviser's office, this dance of delight is tragic. It means, as a client, you never get to what is poignant for you, what is deeply urgent or profound. Money and meaning will never be integrated. The minute the financial adviser interrupts our train of thought, and (more importantly) the movement of our feelings, we have our first insight: "Oh, yes, I remember. This is not about me. This is about them." Or, "It's about financial matters." Or we realize it's about our relationship with the financial adviser, and so we immediately start to take care of that relationship. We begin to censor the things we really want most to talk about, because, well, maybe they don't really belong in a "financial" conversation and at least this adviser doesn't seem open to them or really interested, so maybe it's not safe to talk so personally, so intimately. The second time the adviser interrupts, we give the conversation over to them completely. The meeting is theirs, not ours. We just follow their lead.

But what Alan was most interested in was where Tracey was going, not in sharing his overlapping interests with her, and certainly not in talking about his financial services. He understood that there was an emotional arc to her talk, and the last thing he wanted to do was to interrupt that, or he might never have the chance to be there with her like that again. So instead he facilitated that arc by pauses and the most unobtrusive expressions of appreciation or concern. He knew that only if she got to the end of her feelings would he (and she) know what she really wanted to say and what she really wanted in life, what she wanted her money to make happen. And he knew, in order for her to feel safe getting there, he must be empathic, quiet, connected. He knew that she must deeply understand that above anything else he wanted to hear what she had to say. As a client, you can't do Life Planning with someone you can't trust, and the slightest interruption to our tales of meaning, our tales of aspiration or of woe, tales we often haven't ever spoken to others (possibly for as long as 33 years!), sends a message to us that the adviser is not really interested in hearing why we've come to see them. They're not someone we can trust with who we really are.

When we do the work of Life Planning for ourselves, we will need to be just as open and just as willing to put on the table what we care about most as Tracey and Bill were.

The Challenges of Debt and of Youth

Most Life Planners are financial planners, so it's not surprising that clients want first to talk about their money concerns.

When Jennifer came in for her initial meeting with Bryan Gasparro, an RLP® in Virginia who specializes in middle-income clients, they shook hands and she looked him in the eye with confidence. But all of that show of confidence disappeared quickly when they sat down and he asked the two questions with which he started each Exploration meeting: "Is there anything urgent we need to deal with right away?" and "Why are you here, what would you like to accomplish in our meetings together?"

Jennifer fumbled with her briefcase and nearly fell off her seat, sending some of her papers sailing across Bryan's desk. As they gathered them all together, she looked up at him like a trapped animal and in a shaking voice said, "I hope my situation isn't too much of a mess for you. I've thought about contacting you for some time but I'm embarrassed about my poor credit and huge debt. I'm worried it's too late." Jennifer was 25, with $45,000 in college loans and interest that was no longer deferred.

"It costs me $1,000 a month to pay down the debt," she said. "At this rate, it will take years. My dad gave me $20,000 when I got my degree in exercise science. I don't know what to do with it. Spend it, or save it, or . . . I hate to use all of it to pay off loans. But I want to get financially grounded. I want to do things that are important to me, and not just work to pay bills."

"That sounds exciting," replied Bryan. "Let's talk about the finances toward the end of the meeting. I'd love to hear about what's important to you first."

Jennifer had not allowed herself room to dream, much less to think, consumed as she was by the debt and by long hours paying it off. So she was surprised and noticeably relaxed as Bryan showed a real interest in the things she most wanted to do and to be. It was at this point that Life Planning really began, and that Jennifer and Bryan talked in earnest about her life.

She was a nurse with a passion for fitness. She loved travel, yet also wanted to buy a home and feel settled. Over the course of this initial meeting she designed (with Bryan's encouragement) a professional life that would allow her to intermingle nursing with fitness and travel. It was a vision she'd never put together before, and you could see her energy gather to begin to make it happen. "That would be my dream life," she said. "It would be so exciting!"

Bryan took the last half hour of the conversation to begin to explore Jennifer's layers of debt, her father's gift, her capacity for saving and the funding of her future aspirations, including a home. As homework he asked for more detail on the financials and gave her the Life Planning goal exercises for the Vision meeting. He explained that the purpose of the next meeting would be to further clarify her aspirations and that only once they were clear should she take decisive action on her debt. At the end of the meeting, Jennifer couldn't thank Bryan enough.

Bryan's skill here was in balancing Jennifer's worries, concerns and self-doubt with her aspirations, letting her know that both were important. In a similar way, as you begin working on your own Life Plan, you will want at least as much room for your vision as for your concerns.

Let's look at one more example before we get to work on your own Life Plan.

Financial Concerns and Out of Work

Ben and Anita came in to see Louis Vollebregt, a Registered Life Planner®️ in the Netherlands. Ben, 48, had been laid off from his job as a manager in a retail business. Anita had a part-time job and had stayed at home much of her life to care for their children. They had some retirement savings and they were paying for their children's education, but most of their money was tied up in their home. All their talk was about money. How long did they have till it would run out and they would have to sell their home? What would happen to their retirement savings, and how could they ever retire given the job loss and the need to finish their children's university expenses? What were their financial options, and how much of a safety net did they need? They saw no future for themselves. Ben talked angrily about how he needed to get his job back so he could support his family, and Anita spoke almost in a monotone about how she would need to return to the full-time administrative work that she disliked so much, but knew so well.

Louis gave Ben and Anita all the room they needed to talk from their frustration, anxiety and despair. But as they moved through their emotions, Louis noticed that they began to replace those feelings with a vision of the life they wanted instead.

Anita, 43, enjoyed cross-breeding plants, which she did in her own nursery, and longed for more creativity in her life. Ben spoke of having wanted all his life to be self-employed, but how he always felt constrained financially and was never quite willing to take the risk. Louis let them know that Ben's loss might be a blessing in disguise, and that from his brief glance at their financial situation he thought they could get much closer to the life they dreamed of than they had ever thought possible.

"I've got some goal exercises I'd like you to do in preparation for our next meeting. In the meantime, the more you can suspend your disbelief and envision a really great future, the more productive our time will be."

Ben and Anita were obviously moved by the conversation. They had experienced the first step of the process that would shift them from financial despair toward a future that contained both hope and action. In acknowledging the worst of their current situation, they had turned a corner, gained confidence in themselves as well as Louis, and were ready for the next steps.

In Exploration, we clear the decks. Financial concerns are put to the side, emotions are moved through until we can see what is possible, until we can dream again. And then we can look at what we want from life. We put it all on the table.

Much more comes out of an Exploration meeting than I can convey in a few pages of text. Friendships, hobbies, illnesses, jobs, homes, secret sorrows and delights, generations of family stories, aspirations, frustrations, travel, disappointments, mentors, values, possessions, creative pursuits, gardening, sports, entertainments, obligations, as well as finances. Because Life Planners hold themselves back from the conversation in order to be sympathetic and appreciative listeners, the "conversation" follows exactly the arc of meaning the client longs to share. There's really nothing like it. Everything comes pouring forth. Very often it is the last things shared that are the most meaningful, that the client has most longed to bring forth.

As clients of Life Planners we trust, often for the first time, we have someone on our side, not merely interested (as a friend might be) but committed to delivering us into the life that we have always wanted to live, and skilled at putting the financial architecture in place to make it all work.

How can we do this work ourselves, without an adviser? Let me share some thoughts with you.

Self-Help

Most Life Planners, and certainly all Registered Life Planners®, have been trained in listening skills, trained to listen very carefully to what you say, as if it were a profound music. Among the most important structures in the music they are listening to are the melodies of your inspirations and delights and how they are intertwined with the dissonance of your frustration, doubt, anxiety and despair. Life Planners have been taught to respond empathically to your concerns and with engaged and appreciative interest to your aspirations. They are trained to listen to you, but begin their training by listening first inside themselves, first for sensations, then for feelings, finally for the differences between thoughts and feelings. When a person has received this training they are a much better listener because they're listening with their whole being, all their senses; they are more tuned in to your emotional tones and the emotional tones of the conversation. They know where you are. The realm of possible miscommunications is reduced dramatically and there is greater integrity in your relationship. They are all the more easily dedicated to your success as they are connected with you in an authentic and meaningful way. They don't interrupt with their concerns, their spreadsheets, their own ideas, their agenda, until you are complete with everything that is important for you to say. So how can we give to ourselves this quality of listening that we might receive from a Life Planner?

One of my teachers once told me that "speech is already two stages removed from the truth of things." He never explained what he meant, and I'm embarrassed to say it took me years to figure it out. If I'm right, it's very simple. Before speech there is thought, and before thought there is the deeper space of intuition, of feeling and sensation, and of consciousness itself. One might even say, of spirit. I suspect it is this that Life Planners access inside themselves in listening training. If, as we begin our own exploration, we were to tap into this pre-conscious space, our own exploration of what must be included in our marriage of meaning and money will be more complete. Let's take a moment to listen to ourselves, before we begin to bring our thoughts into action and onto pages, charts, designs and the web.

Some of you may be put off by this kind of inner listening. If you are, feel free to skip these next two paragraphs and move on to action in the following one. Some of you already have an inner listening practice of meditation or prayer. Feel free to go to that place to begin this exploration. Otherwise you might start like this: find the quietest place you can, untroubled by cell phones or door bells ringing, untroubled by insects or pets. Sit comfortably, but with the back relatively erect, the shoulders at ease, eyes closed and with a gentle breath. Moving with your awareness from the base of your posture upwards, pause in each location where you feel the sensations of the body or of emotions. Notice gently, softly, even tenderly exactly how they feel – their dimensionality, their temperature, their texture, their qualities of movement and how they are changing. Be interested, even intrigued in how they are conveying meaning to you, without adding thoughts. In fact let go of every thought as it arises, and return to this careful inner listening.

With feelings, note every emotional tone and how it's configured in the body. If it's connected to a particular emotion that you can name, note it as well. Keep letting go of thoughts. Do this practice until you feel very present with all that is inside you, or very quiet. For some of you that will just take a few minutes, for others it may take ten or twenty. I've written in depth about this process and other practices that extend and support it in my book *Transforming Suffering into Wisdom: The Art of Inner Listening* (2010).

Start with a Wildly Open-Ended Approach

As you emerge from inner listening, see if you can access qualities inside you of acceptance, patience, equanimity and openness, and then of interest, appreciation and optimism. This will prepare you both to access and affirm everything that comes up as you reflect and write down (or record) whatever you can think of, financial or not, that you would like to accomplish, or that you would like to discuss if you were entering a genuinely empathic and interested Life Planner's office – the office of someone you might think of as a mentor.

So try that. Start with a wildly open palette. The very best way to do this is to go to my free consumer Life Planning website, www.lifeplanningforyou.com, where I guide you through the EVOKE® process on pages of your own creation, password protected, and where you can revisit or revise your thoughts from any place in the world anytime you want. It is an ideal companion site to this book. (Note: To gain access to the website for the first time, please log-in and register.) So, ideally on the website, or if not, with journal or computer, write down everything that comes to mind that you might like to accomplish, have, be or do. Write down the practical tasks that need to be sorted. Note the feelings associated with each item. List the roadblocks as well.

If you use mind-mapping software, this is an ideal exercise for it, again starting with a wide-open palette. You can write things, but also bring in photographs, bits of music or film, links to articles that are relevant, and anything else that comes to mind and the software allows.

Highs and Lows

In the Exploration meeting, when the open-ended conversation is complete, the Life Planner looks at the emotional highs and lows that have emerged in the conversation, what really excited the client, what brought anxiety or discouragement. They do this to let the client know they can be there in the fullest range of the client's aspirations and concerns. Likewise for you, nothing should be too "out-there" aspirationally or emotionally. Everything that's important to you, make sure it's addressed. Then, of all the things you listed, elaborate on the things that excited you the most, and the things that most concerned you. Finally, in the following chart list the aspirations and concerns that have the greatest meaning for you in the Meaning column, and then the financial aspirations and concerns in the Money column.

Money, Meaning, Aspirations, Concerns Chart

	Money	Meaning
Aspirations		
Concerns		

Take the items where you feel most inspired, or the areas to which you are most deeply and profoundly moved and gently let yourself know that you can do these things, you can accomplish them, you can create the time for them. Give yourself reassurance where you have doubts. Let yourself know that Life Planning itself will bring you through. Add these thoughts and reflections to your notes.

If you want, write down positive affirmations of kindness or accomplishment around each of these areas.

Then take the most emotionally troubling areas and kindly, gently let yourself know that you can handle these areas, you can address them, that as part of Life Planning, you can get through them. Gently imagine how that might be, and add those thoughts to your notes.

Your Financials

An Exploration meeting is not merely an open-ended conversation. It has financial elements to it as well. Often in an office setting, the conversation begins with any urgent questions you might be bringing to the meeting. Typically you would have brought your financial documents with you, and by the end of the meeting, your Life Planner would have addressed your urgent questions and also identified any additional documents you might bring to the following meetings. They would also begin to look at and comment on your basic economic situation.

We'll do that work in Knowledge, a few chapters away, where we give you financial road maps and guide you to financial resources. For now it is enough to have listed your financial concerns and aspirations, and to know they will be addressed as part of your Life Plan.

Exploration begins your Life Plan. Putting all your thoughts down on paper or using our free consumer website, www.lifeplanningforyou. com, is just the beginning. It's like writing a book. We've gathered all the materials, we've begun to know many of the characters and the scenes and to sense the purpose of it all, but the crafting of the work, its sense of proportion, its depths and its denouement remain yet to be explored.

Trust the process. You will be surprised how far it will take you. If you get blocked doing this yourself and want some help, keep in mind I will help you find a Life Planner you can trust. A mentor can often help us cut through subtle layers of lethargy that trap us around money. He or she can also help facilitate decisions couples make relating to money, areas fraught with danger and divorce.

If you find this work exciting or challenging, it wouldn't surprise me. Here are some of the comments we hear in an Exploration meeting: "I realize for the first time how messages I've carried about money for decades have been blocking me, and I think I'm ready to let them go." "I never imagined how helpful it would be to bring my life into a conversation about money." "I've always made all the financial decisions. I never realized how important it was to have my spouse as partner in all this." "I've never felt so relaxed, so hopeful or so inspired around money before." "This was simply one of the best conversations I've ever had. Thank you so much for this."

I hope this has been a good beginning for you. In the next section, Vision Exercises, you will come to two of the most inspirational exercises in Life Planning. These begin to make the bridge into the Vision phase that I will describe in the next chapter. If Exploration hasn't done it already, these exercises will launch you into your Life Plan, and provide the richest material for visioning those things that will fill your life with meaning.

Vision Exercises

As you might guess, Life Planning hinges on our individual responses to profound and provocative questions challenging us to look at how close we are to living what would be most meaningful, passionate and exciting for us. It works only if in response to these questions, whether on our own or with a mentor/guide (RLP®), we make a vital and vigorous decision to live the life we most long to live. There are a variety of exercises we use to provoke a response like this. Two of the best follow: The Three Questions and Ideal Days vs. Current Days.

The Three Questions

These are the questions I've become famous for. I used them in my financial practice for 30 years, and in my workshops. I first introduced them internationally in *The Seven Stages of Money Maturity* (1999). They are now being used by financial advisers on six continents. I will describe the questions as well as the process in greater detail later, but for now, as you consider these questions, write down your responses.

It will greatly help the creation of your own Life Plan, as well as your understanding of EVOKE® and the Vision phase, if you go to the website, www.lifeplanningforyou.com, and complete your responses to

The Three Questions. There you can create a digital version of your own Life Plan. Optionally, you may use paper or a computer instead.

It is best if you complete your entire response to Question One before even reading Question Two, and equally important that you finish Question Two before considering Question Three.

Question One

I want you to imagine that you are financially secure, that you have enough money to satisfy all of your needs, now and in the future. The question is . . . how would you live your life? Would you change anything? Let yourself go. Don't hold back on your dreams.

Would you change your life and how would you do it?

Question Two

This time you visit your doctor who tells you that you have only 5 – 10 years left to live. The good news is that you won't ever feel sick. The bad news is that you will have no notice of the moment of your death. What will you do in the time you have remaining to live? Your finances remain as they currently stand.

Would you change your life and how would you do it?

Question Three

This time your doctor shocks you with the news that you have only one day left to live. Notice what feelings arise as you confront your very real mortality. Reflecting on your life, both all your accomplishments to date and all the things that you will leave unfinished or undone, ask yourself:

What did I miss?

Who did I not get to be?

What did I not get to do?

Usually answering these questions is inspiring, impelling a person to accomplish what is most meaningful in their life. Occasionally the questions can be dispiriting, as the person realizes how far they are from accomplishing what matters most and how little attention they have given it. In both cases, it is the purpose of this book to show you how to take your responses and turn them into inspired action, how to accomplish your dreams and be living the life you most value. In fact, we will do that with you very shortly, over the next few chapters.

Ideal Days

An additional exercise I recommend is the following. What I'd like you to do is create a schedule that would be absolutely ideal for you, assuming for the sake of this exercise that you have all the financial resources to live as you like. What would your ideal (but typical) day look like, from the moment you awake till the moment you go to sleep? See if you can do it hour by hour. Waking up to cappuccino, sleeping in, taking a walk on the beach, whatever it is! This is meant to be an ideal day, but not necessarily a vacation day. You may choose to work, if you so desire, but the hours are your own.

Then do the same with your ideal week, paying particular attention to the weekends. How might they differ from your ideal days?

Once you've finished the ideal day and week, I'd like you to make a calendar of your ideal year. You know, skiing in the Alps in January, a New England trip in October, a cabin on a pond in the summer. Whatever it is. Don't hold back. What would it be like if it were ideal, and where would you be?

Fill in the charts on the following pages or create your own, larger versions on paper or using a computer.

Ideal Day

Please describe hour by hour, how you would spend your ideal day - each day of your life - if you had all the resources you need to live exactly as you would like.

5 AM	
6 AM	
7 AM	
8 AM	
9 AM	
10 AM	
11 AM	
12 PM	
1 PM	
2 PM	
3 PM	
4 PM	
5 PM	
6 PM	
7 PM	
8 PM	
9 PM	
10 PM	
11 PM	
12 AM	

Ideal Week

Please describe hour by hour, how you would spend your ideal week- each week of your life- if you had all the resources you need to live exactly as you like.

	Monday	Tuesday	Wednesday	Thursday	Friday	Saturday	Sunday
5 AM							
6 AM							
7 AM							
8 AM							
9 AM							
10 AM							
11 AM							
12 PM							
1 PM							
2 PM							
3 PM							
4 PM							
5 PM							
6 PM							
7 PM							
8 PM							
9 PM							
10 PM							
11 PM							
12 AM							

Ideal Year

Please describe month by month, how you would spend your ideal year- each month of your life- if you had all the resources you need to live exactly as you like.

January	
February	
March	
April	
May	
June	
July	
August	
September	
October	
November	
December	

Current Days

Now write down, with unflinching realism, how your life actually is, day by day, week by week, year by year. Don't hold back. Much of the point of the exercise is to contrast your "ideals" with your current reality.

Fill in the charts on the following pages or create your own, larger versions on paper or using a computer.

<u>*Current Day*</u>

Please describe hour by hour, how you spend your typical day

5 AM	
6 AM	
7 AM	
8 AM	
9 AM	
10 AM	
11 AM	
12 PM	
1 PM	
2 PM	
3 PM	
4 PM	
5 PM	
6 PM	
7 PM	
8 PM	
9 PM	
10 PM	
11 PM	
12 AM	

Current Week

Please describe hour-by-hour, how you currently spend your typical week.

	Monday	Tuesday	Wednesday	Thursday	Friday	Saturday	Sunday
5 AM							
6 AM							
7 AM							
8 AM							
9 AM							
10 AM							
11 AM							
12 PM							
1 PM							
2 PM							
3 PM							
4 PM							
5 PM							
6 PM							
7 PM							
8 PM							
9 PM							
10 PM							
11 PM							
12 AM							

Current Year

Please describe month-by-month, how you currently spend your typical year..

January	
February	
March	
April	
May	
June	
July	
August	
September	
October	
November	
December	

Now contrast them, the "currents" with the "ideals." Are they very much alike, totally different, or just different in degree? How do you feel about the differences? Does the gap feel impossible to close, or are there clear and obvious ways to immediately and dramatically improve your life?

Simple changes in the structure of your week can make a huge difference. Reed Fraasa, RLP®, is a good example. Reed was having trouble implementing his Life Plan. He was working long hours five days a week, yet he never seemed to get his work done and meet his goals. He was frustrated that his two big goals – time with his family and time for his writing – were being compromised. So he did something radical. He simply stopped working one day a week in his business, cutting his work week from five days to four. Suddenly his time was much more productively spent. Reed actually accomplished more in four days than he had in five, and was able to put significant time into the family and writing that were at the core of his Third Question. How did he manage this? He was challenged to work more efficiently and he accepted the challenge. That challenge, plus the reward of doing what he loved with an extra day each week, put his passion to work, and created a vigor he had not realized was possible.

Shining a critical light on our ideal life and contrasting it with our current reality challenges us to bring more of the ideal into our current life – virtually immediately. They speak to us in such a persuasive way that we start to live a much happier and richer life right now, and we are inspired to take creative measures, as Reed demonstrated when he cut his work week to four days and enjoyed much more vigor and productivity as a result.

In Vision, the next chapter, we will expand upon each of these exercises and add more. There you will identify, richly describe and begin to live the life that you most long to live, and to which your Life Plan will be aimed.

Vision - EVOKE®
Where the Torch is Lit

There is a moment in Life Planning when the person being planned comes alive. We call that moment "Lighting the Torch." It is a thrilling moment for most people. It's the moment when we realize the dream we have held onto all our lives is achievable – and in short order. It can also be a terrifying moment, as it is when we realize sometimes with a clap of thunder that without action on our part, our most precious dreams might slip away.

It can also be the most touching of moments. It is not unusual for couples to recognize in poignant ways the reasons they love each other. Sometimes relationships that have been strained begin to ease, and the couple starts to fall in love again. At other times, in the midst of this intimacy there can be moments where even the Life Planner is challenged by what seems to be a great gulf between the dreams of one spouse and another, as I experienced with Timothy and Mary.

They came to see me when I was still in the early years of my career as a financial planner, still wet behind the ears and long before I put the name of Life Planning to the work that I did. To me, EVOKE® was just how I did financial planning, not yet a formal system.

Timothy, in his mid-50s, was feeling washed up at work. He had accumulated some retirement money as well as some savings, and wanted to see if there was even the remotest chance he could retire early. He was both doubtful and quite anxious about it all. Mary, a few years younger, had raised the kids and ten years earlier started a garden shop in a Boston suburb. Her business was small but highly regarded for the quality and unusual nature of its plants. This much I had learned in their Exploration meeting two weeks earlier. I'd also had a glance at their cash flow and net worth statements, and the retirement package that Timothy could expect. I'd learned that Mary, who had no desire to retire, had been a librarian before she started the garden shop, that Timothy loved sailing, Mary loved gardening, and they both loved their grandchildren.

Timothy was good at figures, and was quite nervous because he thought he needed another five years or more of work. His nervousness was close to despair; he was that unhappy at his job. Although we spent little time on these figures in the initial meetings, I appreciated his calculations and could see his concern. But I also saw that he completely ignored Mary's earning capacity in his calculations, and had undervalued the contributions Social Security and small inheritances might make. It was not the right time to discuss those details. We were in the Vision phase of the engagement, not Obstacles or Knowledge where all the concerns are worked out and a plan is delivered. Also, he might have objections to my thoughts that for the time being would rob us of our ability to light his Torch.

I've learned that it's always best to follow the EVOKE® process quite precisely. A strong Torch will burn through many an obstacle that a strong argument won't. With a weak Torch you can't even see the path. With my knowledge of finance I could see light where Timothy saw only a tunnel of darkness, but for this meeting, I did not try to convince him of that. Instead I asked him to park his concerns off to the side for now, promising that we would address them.

Most often when I work with couples, I start my work focusing on the one who seems less dominant in the conversation and in the formulation of goals. Although there was a lot of balance and give and take in their relationship, I would normally have started with Mary. In this case, seeing the state of Timothy's concern, even anxiety, after a few moments of chit-chat I broke that custom and started with him. In his agitated condition, he wouldn't have been able to pay attention to Mary.

"First off I want to thank you both for sending me your responses to the goal exercises last week. I often don't receive them till this meeting, so it was great to have a chance to review them before you came in, and I just want to say how wonderful they all are! And how great it is for me as a planner to work with a couple that has so many overlapping interests. I mean family, and reading, and the love of nature that practically rings off each of your pages."

Timothy and Mary exchanged warm glances and then look back at me.

"And I'm wondering if it would be alright, Timothy, with all your concerns about your work and your hopes for early retirement if I might start our work today with you?"

Timothy looks at Mary, who nods back to him. *"Sure, George, that would be fine."*

"And Mary, would that be alright with you?" "Yes, of course." "Are you sure?" Mary nods.

For the next 20 minutes, Timothy and I lost ourselves in the richness of his dreams, of his passions and delights, in everything that brought him to life – all quite in contrast to what he carried with him everywhere he went these days, and what he had shared with me in our first meeting, a work life that he dreaded, and hours, days, weeks, months and years in which he felt he was wasting away. In our first meeting much of my work had been to bring empathy and bits of encouragement to Timothy, but in Vision I work mostly with the qualities of appreciation, excitement, optimism, inspiration and delight. I want to help build the fire, and it was astonishing (and yet simply part of the process) to see how quickly he dropped his concerns when he talked about the things that interested him and how much he came to life. I was also pleased to note how often Mary smiled with appreciation, or chuckled with encouragement.

We had gone over each of Timothy's answers to Question One and Question Two, as well as all his responses to the other goal exercises and were zeroing in on Question Three.

"So Timothy, what's extraordinary to me, with all the many-layered richness of your responses to the exercises so far, is that in your answer to Question Three you only say one thing. It's not unheard of, in my experience,

although it is more common for clients to have three to five responses or even more. When I see just one thing, it always means that it's something extremely important.

Timothy nodded.

"If you recall, the question asks you to imagine that, due to a rare and unexpected ailment, you have discovered that you only have one day left in your life. It asks you to reflect on all the things that you have accomplished and all the things that will remain undone, and to share what it is that you feel that you would miss, that you would not be able to accomplish or that you could not become if you were to die tomorrow. What is astonishing to me, and surprising, is that with all the love and delight you have for so many things, the solitary thing you list here is that you weren't able to spend the rest of your life sailing the world." I paused and felt a lump in my throat as I held Timothy with a steady and compassionate gaze. Before he talked I had time to swallow and to notice the sadness I felt for him, as well as some anxiety as I held this vulnerable moment with him. I did not glance at Mary, but I could feel her hushed anticipation matching my own.

Timothy looked down before I could finish the sentence. With his hands he twisted a tissue to shreds. For the first 15 minutes of our conversation there had been frequent glances at Mary, with lots of shared laughter, but for the last five minutes it was clear that his focus, and our conversation, was all about him. Now, for the lump in his throat, he could hardly talk. He wouldn't look at me as he struggled to speak.

"It's alright," I said, "you can be here." Encouraging him to stay with his feelings, I was silent.

"I've lived all my life for others," Timothy finally said. "I've worked for the family, raised the family; I've given to the community; worked for corporations, always for others, never for me." He gazed up at me mid-sentence, but then choked up again and looked down. I said nothing. I knew that he knew that I was with him. I continued to hold my gaze, gently, kindly. All my focus was on him, and my passionate intention matched my professional one to bring him to the place that he longed most to be, to deliver that as part of the Life Plan. His face was turning red. "God damn it, it's time to do something for me," Timothy said, looking up at me, half-scowling, and then with real conviction, "It's time to do something for me."

Timothy didn't look at Mary, but I could hear her sniffle, and fumble in her purse for tissues.

"Have you ever been called?" Timothy looked up at me as he asked, and for a moment I felt my heart leap and then some tension as I held myself back from sharing how deep that question went for me. It would have been so easy to break Timothy's solitary space, his depth, to do "the dance" with him and start a conversation about our respective callings or even to take the meeting over with my passion.

"I mean like really called. Not just every week, but daily, sometimes hourly, sometimes the smell of the sea, or the sound of the waves or the feeling of adventure and wonder when you pull into a remote evening bay with no signs of human activity to set up camp. Sometimes it's so intense I can't work. I mean it's strange. I'm over 50. It's not like I'm some adolescent with a dream. I'm a man nearing retirement, with my kids gone their own ways. I should be settling in, and here I am longing for that adventure and the place of wonder inside me, the wonder I never had. It's a wonder to me I still have that space inside me, after all I've done." He laughed an almost cynical laugh, but I could tell it was a laugh with the fierceness of determination inside it.

"But I don't know if I'll ever get to do it. I'd love to spend the rest of my life sailing. I don't know if I can afford it, haven't ever talked with Mary about it. And my body. Who knows when the body begins to go?" I could hear his breathing, a measured pace, hardly one of despair, but his concern was evident. "I've got to do it, George. I mean I've got to. Don't know how, but I've got to."

"I agree."

"You do?" he said, with an almost challenging look on his face, as if he couldn't quite believe me, and as if it didn't really matter to him, with only the slightest hint that he would like an ally on this, that it would make him stronger, that it might be just the difference that could make the dream real.

"I do," I responded with conviction, paused and thought for just a moment how I could frame this so Mary could support what I said regardless of her dreams. "In fact, Timothy, if as a consequence of our work together, I or we were able to deliver to you a life rich with sailing, often months at a time, with just the sense of adventure and wonder that you seek so that you can look back at your life by the end of this year and say to yourself: I'm doing it, I'm sailing the

world, I'm living the life I've always wanted, how would that be? How would that feel?"

For the first time in many minutes, Timothy relaxed, he laughed almost in disbelief, a huge smile on his face. "Well that would be incredible!" he exclaimed. "You don't really mean you could do that?"

"That's why you're here, isn't it?"

"Yes, but . . ." he looked at Mary, "how is that possible?"

"Well I've looked at your figures, and I think it is possible. Not without sacrifice, perhaps, but I think it's possible. Would that suit you?"

"Yes, my god yes!" Here Timothy paused, looked down, but with a relaxed face. "We'll have to work this out with Mary."

"Of course, but it's time for you to have your dream. You've been called. It's time to live into that calling."

"Yes, I know." He paused again. "But my resources are small, George. I don't even have a boat. How will we do this? We'll have to work out the finances."

"Absolutely, that's why I'm here, I've looked at your finances. I think you can do it. What's important for now is to suspend your disbelief and live into your dream. We'll tackle the obstacles next week. For now, I'd like you to live into the dream." Pause.

"Wow!" Timothy paused. "Well, let's go! What's next?"

I had plotted out several scenarios in my head from glancing at their cash flow, net worth and retirement figures. I thought without question that if both Mary and Timothy decided to sell their house and their shop and pick up and sail around the world together for the rest of their lives, they had enough equity, savings and retirement to be able to do it, right now. The situation was a bit dicier if they wanted to keep their home in Massachusetts without renting it out, but with Mary's shop equity, eventual Social Security and possible inheritances that might work out as well, or with another year or two of savings it could be more certain. I also didn't have a clue what Mary thought of all this, but they were a loving couple, so I had some trust that it would all work out. The important thing at this moment was to light Timothy's Torch as bright as it could be, bringing vitality and vigor out of his despair, a vitality and vigor that could add tremendous value in its creativity and energy, even financially, to the solution. As I've said, a Torch that is really on fire can blaze through even the most challenging obstacles.

Perhaps Timothy was aware and prepared, but I certainly wasn't, for what came next.

I looked at Mary. She had a sweet, but private smile on her face; didn't quite look at me, as if she too had gone through a lot of feelings in our conversation. After all, it sounded as if Timothy had shared things he'd never quite shared with her before, and we were talking about a new direction in their lives that she quite likely was unprepared for, and yet it looked as if she had found her way to some kind of peace.

"How was this for you?" I asked.

"There's just one thing," she said, not answering my question directly. She paused. "I don't like water. I get seasick."

Just for a moment it flashed before me, a thought I had very seldom in my career. "Oh my god, I've done something wrong." But the panic I felt inside was just for a moment. We were only half way through the Vision meeting. Mary had yet to speak, and I knew there was a lot of love between them. I had to trust it would bring them through. I knew without each Torch alive and blazing brightly, their happiness, their vitality, their health, their fruition and their love were all at stake. I took a deep breath and looked at Mary.

"I've sailed some with Timothy over the years. I know how much it means to him. I was in tears myself, for him, as I heard his calling just now. I remembered how magical those moments were when, together, we would pull into an isolated bay, or when the waters and wind were so still it was like a quiet lake. Climbing the rocks, chopping oysters off them for dinner. Those were my favorite times. And they were special. But I couldn't take the choppy water, the waves, the endless time of them. I got so sick that even a small rocking in the boat wouldn't sit well with me. I tried pills, I tried natural remedies, I tried ginger, nothing worked." She sniffled, blew her nose. "It's his world now, his dream. I want to support him, but I can't be there."

Timothy swallowed, kept quiet. Neither of them could quite look at each other.

I stepped into the middle. "Mary, for now I'd like Timothy to live in the dream, to feel it, taste it, try it out with the greatest possible sense of freedom inside his imagination. I don't know where he will actually settle with it. He might end up doing it part of the year, he might change his mind, he might do it for a year or two and decide that's enough, there may be other things that come up for him that replace it as he realizes that he doesn't need to feel enslaved anymore, that he is a free man. One of the things that is so clear to me from being with the two of you, and from Timothy's answers to the rest of the goal questions is that he loves you and the family dearly. We haven't begun to figure out how all that might play into this. But for now, the best thing for Timothy is to imagine living into his dream, and right now to listen as carefully to yours as you did to his." I paused. She nodded, swallowed. "Are you game?" I asked.

"Yup." Pause. "Let's go."

"So, Mary, assuming all this sailing business of Timothy's works out somehow, in a flourishing way both for him and for you, what are your dreams? What came through for you as you did the various goal exercises?"

"Mostly what I realized, George, was how much I'm enjoying my life just as it is! Quite in contrast with Timothy, I'm afraid, which is part of the reason I want so much for him to feel the freedom he desires. It's quite special to be doing just what you like. Life is really quite wonderful!"

"Ahhh, how great, Mary. I can see how much delight you are taking in your life from your answers to the goal exercises. It was particularly obvious when I saw how your ideal day matches exactly your days as you spend them now."

Mary and I dived into the rich details of her life. I learned a tremendous amount about her business, which was a source of both creativity and excitement for her. She had felt stifled as a librarian, she said, but the business had released her passion for creativity that books teased but never quite fulfilled "on the stacks." The beauty and the ever-changing nature of plant life as well as the creativity of design and her ability to spend time outdoors was invigorating for her, indeed had changed her life. What I noticed also, rare in someone so creative, was that she naturally brought a librarian's understanding of organization, process and structure to the business side of her work, creating a marvelous combination of skills perfectly matched for a boutique business that already commanded a niche market.

I learned also of her daughter and son, her two grandchildren, her parents, and her love of doing simple things with each and all of them. I learned of her love of singing and travel and books. When we came to the Third Question, I paused with her, reflected once again on all the great qualities and things that made up her life, and then began, "It's interesting how in the Third Question this all gets distilled down to what means most, what is richest or most profound or might possibly represent a legacy. Sometimes there are surprises, clarifications. After all the excitement of the things you have just shared with me, I am quite moved by the simplicity of your answer. Do you remember?" (She nodded.) "There are just three things."

"The first thing you wrote was 'Didn't get to grow old with Timothy.'"
Pause.

Mary looked down, lump in her throat, tear in her eye. "We really have a wonderful life. It's not always easy, but somehow I think I've loved every minute of it. I'm looking forward to it being simpler, in some way, for both of us and just enjoying simple things together every day, but not just yet, not right now. I'm happy with Timothy. I don't want to lose him. And I'm loving the thrill of my business."

"Ah, that comes through in other places, your business, but it's curious it doesn't come through here, in the Third Question, where often our legacies come clear."

"Well, that's because I don't think of it in that way. It's not a legacy issue for me, it's just something that I enjoy right now, that keeps me alive in an exciting way."

"I see. Does that mean that growing old with Timothy is a deeper kind of goal?"

"Well, yes. It's the completion of the life we have lived together. I would deeply regret losing that opportunity. I wouldn't want it any other way."

Pause. I didn't look at Timothy or speak for him, but I did think if he was anything like me, he was sitting there with a lump in his throat too. "Anything else?"

"Nothing that I haven't written."

"OK. Would it be alright if I went to your second answer?"

"Sure."

"You just have one word. It must convey a lot. 'Gardening.'" Pause.

"Well, yes. It conveys everything to me. It's a bit of everything. I mean I love the action, being on my knees, digging in the earth, digging up the earth, planting, weeding, working with my tools, and just as much I love the contemplation, the experience in all seasons of what the garden is. All of nature and all my senses are equally alive. I love the quiet of it as much as the action. It's a contemplation I can relax into, and then charge out of with my next new project, with what needs to be done in the moment. It's the one thing I would like more time for, if my business weren't so busy. I suppose when I die, I'd just as soon be gardening, although of course I'd like my family around."

"Wow!"

"Yes, I think it's why my shop does so well. I love everything about it, so people come in, and they know from what we offer and how we respond that we "get" where they're coming from. And that brings up something else that gardening conveys to me. Nearly as much as being in my own garden, I love being in other people's gardens. There's something deep and earthy and active about my own. In another's I come alive with new possibilities, seeing things that they have done, and imagining new ways I might work or new visions I might share with my customers. There's nothing quite like being in a great garden like Sissinghurst, pausing, sitting, contemplating in each of the spaces what a great gardener like Vita Sackville West has created, breathing in the aromas coming off the fields and water that surround it."

"How exciting! So, it sounds as if you'd be willing to travel to experience a great garden."

"You bet. I can't imagine a better vacation, especially if I were to have family nearby."

"Well that makes me think that maybe there's a way to work out Timothy's sailing wanderlust with you, but let's come back to that, because it also brings to mind your third and final response to the Third Question. Can I go there?"

"Sure."

"Brendan and Gaynor. That's it. You're a woman of few words."

"My grandchildren."

Pause.

"It's just, they're so much fun to be with, so alive, and I would miss not experiencing them growing up, not being able to be a grandma to them, not baking something special for them or taking them somewhere special. We're

lucky we live so close. I see them several times a week, often for a day at a time. I had kids early, and so has Christine, my daughter, so I could almost be a mom to them, if it weren't so much fun being grandma."

"So Mary, if as a consequence of our work together I or we could deliver to you the opportunity and the most wonderful possible setting for you and Timothy to grow old together. If we were to deliver also more time daily in your garden to do the simple things you love, and in other gardens monthly or quarterly, gardens that you always wanted to visit but never imagined being in, gardens among the best in the world, and along with this, more time with Brendan and Gaynor, special times, unusual times that they and you might remember for the rest of your life and all of this starting right now, how would that be?"

Mary, with warmth and a big smile, "George, that would be marvelous, icing on the cake. That would really make something special, and begin the second half of my life just the way I want it to be! Now if I can just get this lug to stay home enough to make it all happen!" She smiled at Timothy, and he returned the smile.

"Well," I confessed, "I've got some ideas about that I normally wouldn't bring up till the next meeting, but let me suggest a way of approaching the differences in your visions, something you might take home and contemplate or work on. Would that be alright?"

Both Mary and Timothy nodded positively and with curiosity. "That would be great."

"So, in our next meeting, we'll be dealing with obstacles to the goals you've both identified. I'd like you to leave the obstacles till then, and focus in the meantime on strengthening your visions. One way I could see working on a vision that is mutually acceptable, even possibly delightful, would be for Timothy to consider his goal taking place in stages. The first stage, this year, would be for you to dedicate just three months to sailing, try it out, see how you do, get all the equipment down, the routines, in preparation for a longer launch the following year. And to see how you and Mary do with it. You could view your times at home and ashore with Mary as family time and time also to be preparing for your next adventure. Mary, when you mentioned Sissinghurst, it made me think that you might consider flying in to join Timothy at your favorite ports, ones near gardens. Sissinghurst itself isn't far from the south coast of England, if Timothy were to sail in that direction, and is just a stone's throw from Gatwick. You might consider bringing along with you Gaynor or Brendan to make it extra special. These are just my thoughts, you may be much more creative with yours. But are you game for something like this."

They looked at each other just for a moment, eyebrows raised, with some relief and amusement in their expression.

"Well if we're going to consider Sissinghurst, I'd like to throw in the gardens in Cork. I've always wanted to visit them," suggested Mary.

Timothy was engaged. "I don't know," he said, "the west coast of Ireland can be awfully challenging until the bay at Dingle. I've been thinking about China. I've heard there are wonderful gardens in Shanghai. Or how about Desolation Bay up near Vancouver Island? It can be still as a pond out there."

"Oh, dear, I'd love to go back to Dingle, and don't forget Brendan and Gaynor have relatives near Cork."

"I think you're on to something, George."

"Great! I can't wait to hear your thoughts when you come in next time. And we'll get to work on the obstacles, financial and all. I think we can do this, and look forward to the adventure with you."

In Exploration, nearly everything is brought out onto the table. We become comfortable with it all, open to it often in ways that we have longed for but truly missed, frequently for decades, sometimes for all our life. Often everything is brought forth. But it's not unusual for something deep, something powerful to suddenly appear for the first time in Vision, to arrive in the Third Question, or in the Heart's Core exercise, or to be blurted out in the interview process in a way that says "This is it. If I don't achieve this, I haven't done anything in my life."

In Timothy's response to Question Three, it's not the sailing that's important, but wanting to do it "for the rest of my life." That says it all. I had no idea if Timothy would actually act on his statement, or exactly how sailing would appear in his Torch. What I did understand was that this was the most passionate statement I'd heard from him. It was what told me we were near the Torch. Passion is everything in Life Planning. It's what frees us to be the most brilliant, the most creative, the most authentic person we are destined to be. Without it, we're a pale shadow of who we *really* are. It's what brings us alive, it's what tells us what's worth living for, it reveals where our genius is and where we are to go if we are to thrive, not just survive.

Genius comes alive in Vision. It catches fire in the moment of inspiration we call "Lighting the Torch." Vision is different from Exploration in this way. Exploration is about comforting waters, spreading wide, and allowing all things to enter. Out of those waters, like a phoenix shooting skywards from its ashes, arises the flame of our inspiration that is Vision. Without it, no passion, no action, no brilliance. With it, nothing and no one can hold us back. We don't hold back from the passion in Vision, we don't compromise, no half measures. That's the general rule. There are exceptions, but they are small and insignificant compared to the general rule. I'll talk about some of them in a moment, but for now and in general, in the Vision phase we assume that our dream *has to be realized*.

So we're going to get Timothy sailing right away. Fast enough that he really believes his Torch is possible. As an adviser, I will back him 100%, and not even hint at the obvious compromises that he will have to make to accommodate his current lifestyle, absent his dreary job. He will find the right balance in his own time. For now he needs the fire. Sometimes when we've been held back for so long we need to swing all the way to the other end of our spectrum in order to believe that freedom is really possible. That's what Timothy needed. If he felt it was only half possible, he wouldn't feel free. What is 50% of freedom? It's still slavery.

Vision is about experiencing the rising energy of freedom inside of us so powerfully that we begin immediately to take the steps that will bring us there. I saw a baby bird this morning for the first time leap from its nest and take flight. It's that amazing sense of exhilaration mixed with wonder that comes with flying and exploring our new world. Vision should deliver that. As a client you should experience it with your Life Planner. As a self-help reader, I will help you identify what it is from among the exercises that will give you that exhilaration, and then I will help you make it happen.

Some of you will be wondering how I can justify going with the passion of Timothy to sail the world for the rest of his life, and ignore the deep longing of Mary to grow old with him. This is one of the few areas where the formula of "going with the dream" necessitates modification. Where a dream is dependent on another person, as Mary's is, all a Life Plan can do is help to create the environment in which the person's dream will come alive, or help to facilitate a closing with the dream that will allow access to other passions. So if you want a child, if you want to find the perfect relationship, or if you want to grow old with someone, the best your Life Plan can do is create the most ideal environment for those possibilities to take place. And the wisest set of actions in a Life Plan will be to focus both on the external circumstances and on the internal environment inside yourself that would best facilitate the dream. For instance, if you're single and you're longing for a great relationship, the Life Plan might include (externally) attending events where you come alive and where you might meet someone with similar interests. It might also include (internally) reflections on (or work on) yourself, followed by implementing changes or practice that might make you a better partner.

If your Third Question is all about someone who has died, a spouse or a child that you wish were still alive, there is likely to be a cloud over your life until you can find some kind of closure. That cloud will hold you back from envisioning a life of meaning and passion. It will deny you your freedom to live fully. Your Torch will need to include some actions that will resolve the loss of your old relationship. They could take any number of forms, including visiting favorite places as a way of recalling and saying goodbye. They could include asking forgiveness, writing a letter, creating a song or a film that conveys all that needs to be said. They might include a gift to a favorite charity, or setting up a trust, if you had the funds, or gathering all the old friends together again and saying goodbye in community. My brothers and I gathered together for an afternoon, absent our spouses and children, at the tenth anniversary of our mother's untimely death. It allowed each of us to speak in ways we never could have imagined before about her influence on us, even years later, and about our feelings.

In Mary's case, she already has many things going for her. She has a great relationship with Timothy. They love each other dearly. She's intrigued with the adventure of flying to exotic locations to meet up with him. They share a love of books, and a love of their family and of family events. They have a long and loving history. And Timothy's dream is not to leave Mary, it's simply to sail. He would be delighted if she could join him. And then there is time, time for them both to see how this new world will work for them, or won't! For an adviser in this space, it can require a lot of courage simply to let time unfold.

As it happened, Timothy and Mary had a great first year or year and a quarter, to be exact. I'll fill you in on how they dealt with their obstacles in the next chapter, but at the end of 12 months. Timothy sailed off for three months on his own. Mary flew into a couple of the ports, once with other members of the family in tow, and studied the great gardens in the parts of the world she visited. At the end of the three months Timothy and Mary came in for a quarterly review, and Timothy said to me: "You know George, that was wonderful, the trip of a lifetime, something I will never forget and hope to repeat in some variety for many years. But the truth is, three months a year is about as much time as I want to spend away from Mary, my family and my home. I'm delighted with what we've done, but I want to look at other things I might do as well. Do you think I could do that with you?"

Sailing the world was just the beginning of Timothy's new life. It was the experience of freedom that would open him up to whole new worlds of experience and purpose.

Louis Vollebregt with Ben and Anita

Remember Louis Vollebregt's clients Ben and Anita? They'd come in initially filled with despair after Ben lost his job. When they came for the Vision meeting two weeks later, they had completed all their goal exercises. Anita was still concerned. She said she enjoyed thinking about new possibilities but she didn't want to be naïve when what they needed was income.

Louis agreed that income would become a major theme of their work together, but suggested that the best way to find sources of income was to make sure all possibilities were on the table. Often, he said, surprising sources for income develop when we allow ourselves first to explore the things we care about most.

Anita was open to his suggestions and found herself engaged and excited as together they went over every item listed in her goal exercises. Fearful that she would be called in this process to work that bored her, she was clearly overwhelmed when Louis asked, "Anita, if as a consequence of our work together I or we were to deliver to you your own profitable and enjoyable agricultural business, more time with Ben, and the time and money to take regular family vacations, how would that feel?"

To Anita, Louis had described the perfect life.

Ben had come to the meeting in a very different mood from Anita. He had been stimulated by both the Exploration meeting and the goal exercises, and when Louis asked if anything had changed since their last meeting, Ben replied, "A new export idea – awake half the night with it. I know it's crazy. It's not on the forms I filled out, but somehow it puts everything together for me. It feels like the business I want to create."

Louis noted, glancing at Ben's third question, that "create and run my own business" dominated his responses.

"Yeah, I can't get it out of my head. It's a business exporting wine and other exclusive food products to China." Ben spoke for some time and with great animation about his new idea, and when Louis presented it front and central in his Torch, along with a fitness regime that brought Ben back to tennis and to more time with Anita and the kids, Ben responded, "That is more than I dare ask for."

Louis made an appointment for the Obstacles meeting in two weeks time. He gave each of them the specific assignment to live into their newfound dreams over the coming weeks to make their visions rich and vivid with detail while continuing to let the obstacles go. Both seemed eager to engage in this.

The Five Visions

Life Plans, Torches and answers to Question Three tend to congregate around five themes, often overlapping. By far the most common theme they address is family or relationships. The second most common has to do with spirit or values. The third most common are creativity goals, which can include business ventures. The fourth involves giving back to one's community. And the fifth is about a sense of place. It might be about your home or travel, or a longing for the city or the country, or it might involve concern for the planet. If you think about Timothy's and Mary's responses, all five of these categories were in some way included, particularly in the variety of Mary's Torch.

Let's look for a moment at some typical responses to Question Three that fall into these categories:

1. *Family Goals*

The thought of dying tomorrow fills me with profound sadness and regret that I would not be here to comfort and guide my daughter as she grows up, and to add perspective and calm for my wife as she struggles to raise our daughter in optimism and peace.

The chance to really heal my relationship with my son.

Let Justin and Tina know how much they have meant to me and how loved and protected they have always made me feel.

Missed the opportunity for the "Wow!" gathering of my family that they would remember for the rest of their lives and want to recreate for their own children.

Getting to know my father as an adult.

I missed a closer relationship with my sister and her children.

Finding my soul mate, although I hope to have done that.

I would not get to see what kind of men my boys would grow up to be – to see them fall in love, get married, have children. I would not be a part of their lives.

Often people who list strong family goals and values regret that the balance in their lives has veered too much in other directions, and they need to find more time now to work on those values or to create the kind of bond they desire. In that case, the Life Plan and the Torch will move them back to balance, and usually very quickly. As an example, often the "Wow" gathering of the family occurs within a year of the Life Planning meetings. Where closer relationships are longed for, action is often taken within a week and sustained for years, and where closure is required it is often accomplished before the Life Planning meetings are completed.

2. *Spirit and Value Goals*

I would have liked to live a simple life.

Live a deeper spiritual life.

Speak my mind.

A free spirit.

I would regret that I was not nicer to the people around me.

I wish I had developed patience.

Keep my word.

Retreat in a monastery doing meditation.

You might wonder what these responses have to do with money or with a financial plan. This is where we've really missed the boat in the world of money and finance. We've just gone through, in the 20th century, what I call "the century of sales" when it comes to finance and our lives. As a consequence it is hard to imagine what meaning has to do with money. Money, we think, is all about products and spreadsheets (and a word I can't quite think of that is akin to skullduggery!).

In Life Planning there is a marriage of meaning and money, and it becomes clear as we go through the EVOKE® process that virtually everything in our lives is related to money. The most meaningful of our goals are the most critical ones to focus on because they have the most impact on our lives, including our financial lives.

So, for instance, in the list of spirit and value goals, many are about changing our inner lives, becoming freer spirits, speaking the truth, developing patience and kindness or doing spiritual practice. We think that we should be able to change these things just with some kind of mental switch, but in fact each of these changes takes time, focus and dedication. And if we are spending our time and energy in these areas, we will be taking time and energy from other areas. Often those "other" areas include the places where we make our money. That's the first and most obvious connection to our financial situation and to our financial plans.

The second way that these goals affect our money life has to do with their impact on our energy itself, our vigor in all the things we do. To the extent that our deepest goals and longings remain unfulfilled, it is as if a cloud hangs over our lives and every aspect of them is darkened and diminished. Some half-conscious feeling gnaws at us daily that we've not been the person that we could have been, and all of our activities are plagued as a consequence with a certain level of doubt or depression. Don't address your neglected longings, and your work life is as drained by inefficiency, low energy and lack of confidence as every other aspect of your life. Take the time to realize these dreams, and your life becomes a fountain of energy, as we've seen with the doctor who wanted to become a rabbi, and with Timothy who wanted to sail the world.

3. *Creativity Goals*

I did not get to sing the songs I hoped to sing when I was a child.

I didn't get to act or dance enough, or do them as my job.

I'd like to write a science fiction epic.

Create art specifically for digital media.

Make independent films.

I never got to play jazz in clubs.

Be my own boss as part of a dynamic team.

Create an unusual business, integrating local and global concerns.

Accomplish something that has lasting value.

When I started doing financial Life Planning in the early 80's, I was stunned by the passionate drive for creative fulfillment I found in many of my clients. I had felt alone in my personal passion for creative action both in my business and as an artist. I was thrilled to see the variety of my clients' wishes, and their desire to live creative lives.

Financial advisers have tended to avoid these first three areas of family, spirit and creativity. After all, "What do I know about family or relationship issues?" they might say. "The client should go see a therapist." And "Why are they talking to me about how to develop kindness or to do meditation? They should talk with a spiritual counselor. Better get back to the figures and keep this meeting on track!"

Or they make dumb interpersonal mistakes when these passions come up, lacking the listening skills or the understanding to find out what their clients are really about: "Wow! So you like to paint, and you don't have enough money. Let's put this all together. Why don't you go down to Cape Cod on your weekends and paint seascapes. I think they sell for a lot of money down there!"

Life Planners, trained in EVOKE®, understand that these seemingly intangible or non-monetary goals are usually the most important to achieve for a client. Life Planners also know that their appreciation, empathy and curiosity will usually bring out all that is necessary to understand what the client really wants. They are trained to help the client solve the obstacles to the Life Plan themselves, so the Life Planner never needs to become a counselor, a spiritual adviser or an art critic to deliver exactly what the client needs to live their life of greatest meaning and greatest vitality.

It never ceases to amaze me, the impact on a client of being listened to and appreciated for who they most want to be, the impact of identifying their Life Plan. Simonne Gnessen, a Registered Life Planner® in England, co-author of *Sheconomics* (2009) and originator of the Wise Monkey brand of financial coaching, shared this email with me from one of her creative clientele who couldn't sleep the night after her Torch was lit:

"Okay, so I can't sleep and it's 3.15am! Need to take action! I'll get up and write the ideas buzzing in my head down on paper. Already yesterday's session with my financial coach Simonne has become a launch pad for me!

Can I keep the launch pad grounded and continue to live in all my worlds? Can I both get my dreams down on paper and still spin them to their limits and beyond?

I'm listening to the inspirational music of Giovanni Allevi as I write and it makes me realize that everything fits together, there is rhyme and reason for everything. I feel great with the potential for an extraordinary expansion from this work.

For many years I've thought about the unique potential that we each possess. But never before did it touch my own spirit like this, touch it and tug at it. "Let's go!"

What about Question Three? What would I most regret? Big wake-up call! Now I face it head on. The universe is presenting me with gifts I can't let stagnate! No more hesitation. No more holding back.

Something I will hold onto from yesterday is how I want to take that inspiration into my teaching, my dancing, my writing, into everyday life so that it all becomes more magical, joyful and beautiful. Thank you so much Simonne. God bless."

4. Community Goals

Spend time with people who are feeling cut off from the world – elderly, sick.

Develop our community.

Become someone known as doing things for all not just for himself.

I did not get to be a teacher, to make a difference in other childrens' lives.

Own a local business with profits to local charities and the needy.

Philanthropist – supporting special causes.

In the financial planning world, we have traditionally expected "community" to be one of our client's goals, at least for those wealthy enough to provide for more than just their family in their estate plan. But helping our communities is a passion for most of us, rich and poor alike, whether local communities, national or global. This is a fundamental human desire. Life Planning empowers such passions to be enacted immediately by all, to the benefit of the client and community alike, and not simply a legacy in a will by the wealthy alone.

5. *Place and Environment Goals*

Build the house of my dreams, small but exotic.

A home on the water in Maine where the whole family can gather.

Spend time in the sunflower fields of France.

Small detached house in country with outbuildings.

Making trips to Scotland with a camper and kids.

To live so deeply connected with nature that every moment is fresh, sparkling, alive.

I want to live in a great city, Shanghai, Tokyo, Paris, London, New York.

Stop global warming.

The lure of travel is something we see a lot of in Questions One and Two. It drops off just a bit in Question Three, but it's still there, along with other issues of place, such as where and how we want to live. Part of our legacy and of our living meaningful and purposeful lives is intimately connected with how and where we live or visit on this marvelous planet. These are some of the easiest goals for us to work with in our Life Plan, as they are often more tangible than those in the first four categories. We can celebrate the fun of them with our planner and with others in our lives.

Sample Torches

Let's look at some sample Torches and how they arose from Question Three. A client named Rebecca had just three things in her Question Three:

I didn't get to spend more time with my dad.

Looking good in bathing suit and jeans.

Accomplish something that had lasting value.

Rebecca's Torch included more frequent calls and trips to see her dad, but what really excited her was a special trip they would take together, just the two of them, each year to a place in the world that was of special interest to him, and that in some way connected with her passion to accomplish something that had lasting value as well. Her Torch involved looking fabulous in a bathing suit and jeans, of course, with some innovative exercise and diet approaches that she liked. And it involved designing creative projects for her church community, her work, and her personal interests at home, at least one of which she would commit to by year-end to pursue to its completion as "something of lasting value."

Jeremy had five items in his Question Three:

Spend more time with my boys – one on one and as a family.

Doing more things with the people that I value being around.

I didn't get to do a job that I loved.

Contentment.

I would like to help other people feel good about themselves.

Jeremy's responses were all of a piece. He had started his work life as a software specialist in video conferencing, but had never felt really fulfilled there and had never stopped working long hours. In recent years he had become aware of a longing to be a mentor. His Torch included a morning routine of a walk, yoga and meditation where his inner focus would be on personal contentment. The Torch also included finding a job that he loved with lighter hours and considerably more people time with opportunities to mentor and to work with people that he valued being around. He would begin his search at his current place of employment, but the position would be secured without question within 12 months. Starting right away (but sustained by the new job) he would engage with his family, his boys and friends, to spend time more around campfires in the temperate months and frequent walks with friends and family throughout the year.

Self-Help

Although challenging at times, it is generally easy and fun to do the Vision exercises. It can be deeply meaningful to identify what you most want to accomplish in your life. The hardest part is constructing a Torch that brings you alive with the enthusiasm and energy to accomplish it in short order, and that doesn't leave important goals until years in the future to accomplish. Before we look at how to do that, let's make sure the exercises are all done. Two of the three key exercises were introduced to you in the last chapter to prepare you for the story of Timothy and Mary. These were the Three Questions, and the Ideal Day, Week and Year exercises. Often the exercises are given as homework to bring into the Vision meeting. To start this section of the book, it is important that you have completed those exercises as well as The Heart's Core exercise that follows.

Heart's Core Exercise

A good way to prepare to do the Heart's Core exercise is to review your answers to both the Three Questions and the Ideals. I would expect a number of overlaps from those exercises to Heart's Core. At the same time, the exercise can provide surprises that one would never have expected that then become the essence of a Torch statement. So it is best to be as open as you can to new ideas and fresh insights, and to be flexible and loose as you approach Heart's Core.

For some, Heart's Core will be easier and truer than the Three Questions. For others it will clarify your goals in surprising and valuable ways.

Let's look at the chart on the website as well as on the next page as we reflect on how to use it. The first thing to understand is that each of the boxes is meant to have goals in it. What you fill the exercise with are goals. Not that every box has to have a goal. I've seen some very creative responses to the exercise that just have one element in the whole exercise, one answer in one box and all else was blank! But those are unusual. Most of you will find value in having a number of things in each column. Pay more attention to the columns than the rows. We will analyze the results based on what you entered in the Heart's Core column, the Ought To column and the Fun To column, not by what you entered in Have, Do or Be. In fact, the Have, Do and Be rows are merely meant to give you more ideas of what the full range of your responses might be to each of the columns.

The Heart's Core Column: Please fill this column with those goals that you feel are closest to your heart, to your passion. Often there will be overlap with Question Three, but there are likely to be new things here as well. See if you can find a number of elements. The highest number I've seen here is around 30. I've seen as few as one, or even none.

The Ought To Column: Fill this column with all the goals that come to mind that you feel you *should do* or that you *ought to do*. Responsibilities. Often these are not so much things that you are passionate about as that you feel obliged to do. Income taxes come to mind, doing a budget perhaps, cleaning out the garage.

The Fun To Column: Fill this column with the fun stuff. They won't necessarily have the kind of passion or heart in them that the Heart's Core column might have, but they also won't have the sense of obligation that the Ought To column will have. Here might be guitar lessons, a trip to Paris, skydiving, learning Spanish, riding motorcycles. Of course, some of these things might well belong in your Heart's Core column.

See if you can find the things (Have), actions (Do), or qualities (Be) that feel just right. The best place to do this exercise is on our website (www.lifeplanningforyou.com) with its expandable boxes and column, its links to designing your Torch, and its digital security and flexibility. Or you can do it here. Just dive in, have fun with it!

Heart's Core Grid

	Heart's Core	Ought To	Fun To
H A V E			
D O			
B E			

Each of the exercises we do in Vision is designed to get at our goals in a unique way. The Three Questions ask progressively deeper questions, so that at the end of Question Three we find ourselves reflecting on the most meaningful goals for our life. Not that Question One and Question Two are not meaningful. Often they provide much of the texture in our lives, many enjoyable elements that will become part of our Life Plan or already are part of our lives. But nearly always, every single element of the Third Question will be in your Torch, with its likely accomplishment within a matter of weeks or months, and only occasionally as long as a few years away. The danger of the "self-help" version of Life Planning is that it is often difficult for us to imagine accomplishing our dreams so quickly, so we tend to put them off further in the future. This leads to two tragic consequences. One is that we aren't fired up by our goals, so we end up continuing to live uninspired, low energy or unengaged lives. That alone is a terrible consequence. The second consequence is equally bad, and that is that we never achieve our dreams. So, if you're going to do this yourself, you need to guard against both those outcomes, by insisting for yourself that you can accomplish these goals in short order, and then move rapidly on to the execution of your dreams. If you think you can achieve a goal in 15 years, challenge yourself by asking "How can I achieve this goal right now?"

The Ideal Day, Week and Year exercise is delightful. It contrasts the ideal with the current day, week and year, giving us a breezy and fresh way of seeing areas where we don't currently feel free. It allows us to see just how little or how much might be changed to give us the experience of freedom. One of the secrets to constructing a great Torch is to give yourself at least one thing from your ideal day, week or year that you don't currently have. In fact, it is best if you give yourself something from at least two of the charts if not three. For instance, work at home on Fridays, and close up shop half a day early. Or make sure you get to Portugal this year, and walk the kids home from school twice a week.

The Heart's Core exercise adds meaning by dividing our goals into three arenas. First, those closest to our heart and our passion. Second, those we feel an obligation to do. And third, the fun stuff. Usually the Ought To column is getting in our way, taking time that would otherwise bring us joy and vitality and delivering drudge work to us instead. The Ought To column is the ideal column for outsourcing – getting someone else to do our tax returns, hiring some neighborhood kids to clean out the garage – or perhaps shouldn't be done at all (clean the garage?). Occasionally there's something about family in the Ought To column that we're not excited about at this moment. For instance, visiting Uncle Gavin. Some of the family things may show up in the Heart's Core column in a few years when Uncle Gavin's health declines, or we realize how important it is for our children to know him, but usually right now we should watch carefully to see if these things in our Ought To column are robbing us of the joy and vigor with which we want to live our lives and stealing time from our ability to deliver on our most passionate purposes. Often the Ought To column is filled with responsibilities that have embedded in them "structures of suffering," a topic I describe in great detail in my book *Transforming Suffering into Wisdom* (2010).

It's the Heart's Core column that most often deserves to be in our Torch. Second only to the Third Question responses, most elements of the Heart's Core column should be both in the Torch and in the Third Question. In fact, one way to help you prioritize your most important goals, is to ask yourself if there are things in Heart's Core that are not in the Third Question (or vice versa), why? Does that mean that they are less important to you than those goals that show up in both places?

The Ought To column will virtually never have its responses in the Torch statement, but occasionally the Fun To column has something important, even critical. The things to watch out for are the wild energy or the unusual nature of particular Fun To responses. Among those most likely to have these kinds of responses are those who are caregivers, counselors, overly responsible, first-borns, pastors and trust-fund dependents. Typically the Third Question and Heart's Core responses will be wonderful, sincere, earnest. They may include earth and civilization changing goals, great service to the impoverished or unfortunate, but little in the way of fun. Look to see if something in the Fun To column has so much energy, even "wicked" energy in contrast to all the "good" represented in the other columns that it dramatically leaps off the page at you. I'll give you an example.

One of my pro bono clients from many years ago was a pastor in Hawaii, a lovely man, of great service, widely respected, a genuine leader in his community, someone you knew you could always count on, even at the drop of a hat, to be there for you or for the community. His family had lived in Hawaii for several generations, and at one point had significant real estate holdings. Although all of that was virtually gone by the time Roger had finished divinity school, he had been privileged to see parts of the islands very few tourists had ever seen. He was passionate about the preservation of Hawaiian culture, its people and exotic places, and its endangered environments. A lovely man. A pleasure, indeed an honor, to spend time with.

At the same time, I could tell there was something troubling Roger as we began to work together. He seemed tired, something I might well have picked up on a few years earlier, if I wasn't so in awe of his aloha, his generosity of spirit. He talked as if there was something bothering him in terms of money. A pastor doesn't make much money, and I could see that things were tight for him, although by no means dire. I could also see that he had some only half-acknowledged sense of sadness at the losses of fortune in his family over the generations. And the sadness was mixed with a sense of guilt, of having had family wealth when others in the Hawaiian community were so poor. I could see that his drive to be of service came in part out of an enormous desire to give back.

As you might expect, his Third Question and Heart's Core column were filled with noble sentiments and causes. I was personally so moved by them that I was ready with only a cursory glance at his other goals to "Light the Torch" and help this noble man accomplish his great dreams. But there was something in his manner as I approached the Torch that caused me pause. If I recall correctly, I think just for a moment I thought that he was overly self-deprecating, almost with a touch of cynicism or anger around my appreciations of his goals and who he was, certainly with a heavy tone of weariness. It was a lucky moment for us both; Roger might say God given. A spark of intuition, I looked at his Fun To column that I'd hardly glanced at before. Sure enough there was something there that leaped off the page. I don't know why I hadn't seen it *clearly before. It said it would be Fun To "say f*** you to my congregation, and go out into the jungle, live in a jungle hut and meditate for the rest of my life!"*

I dropped everything I was going to do, and brought Roger's attention to his statement. He tried to brush it off as an aberration, weariness at the end of a long day, but his energy as he tried to dissuade me from focusing here spoke volumes. I asked him, in spite of his protestations, to describe for me what that jungle life might be like, to humor me and just fantasize for a few minutes. Before I knew it we were transported hundreds of years into the past, living off the land, hauling water, walking an hour to town, listening to the birds and waterfalls and rhythms of the ocean and the winds, diving deep into the natural spirit of Hawaii in his meditations. I'd never seen him quite like this before. Roger was at peace and energized at the same time, happy as the songs of the birds he was describing, as passionate as the great movements of the surf and as easy as the warm ocean breezes. This was it. This was the Torch. And yet at the same time I could tell he could never give up his life of service. He was compelled to give – so much so that it was impossible for him to imagine giving back to himself.

So that was my task. As we talked it became clear that three months a year in the jungle would give him all the inspiration he would need to go full bore the other nine months for his community. It created a balance of energy and rhythm, not to mention meaning, in his life that he could embrace passionately.

His Torch included rich and vivid elements from each of these two periods of his life. At first Roger questioned whether he could afford to take that much time off a year, and whether his church community would support his need for spiritual renewal and spiritual practice. He guessed, though, that they could find from a rich community of fellow pastors around the world, some, possibly retired, who might give their eye-teeth to be able to dedicate their summers to serving his congregation in Hawaii, while he took himself to the jungle.

I could go into the details of how we worked this out for Roger, but that is not a tale of Vision, but one of Obstacles, Knowledge and Execution. What is important here is that you look honestly at your own life and your responses to the goal exercises, and see if there is anything in the Fun To column that stands out in an extraordinary way, anything that needs to be included somehow in the Life Plan and the Torch that inspires you to live your Life Plan.

This is a tough one. I talked to Roger recently, told him about this book and about the web-based application site I was looking to create for those who didn't want an adviser, wanted to do it all themselves. With some scorn in his voice, "I never could have done that with a computer," he said, "not what you did with me." The hardest thing, as you attempt to do this yourself, is to see your blindspots, your unconscious responses, your ways of hiding from yourself what would be truly meaningful and exciting, the way your excuses don't hold water, the elephants in the room. All of that on one side, and then on the other side seeing clearly what your limits, particularly financial, really are. It is my goal to prove Roger wrong, through everything I do here in the book and in the web application I've created. In fact I believe the book and website offer some ways to improve upon what I did with him.

Let's see how you might create a *great* Torch statement for yourself! And please visit www.lifeplanningforyou.com to see how we do this and "paint the picture" online.

How to Construct and then Light Your Torch

1. First of all, include everything that you've listed in the Third Question.

2. Second, include nearly everything (if not everything) in the Heart's Core column.

3. Third, from the Ideal Day, Week and Year pages, include at least two items, preferably from at least two of the three exercises.

4. Look in the Fun To column, in Questions One and Two and also the "Aspiration/Meaning" box in the Exploration chapter for anything that feels essential, deep or wild with energy that has been ignored.

5. Put in time frames that excite (and possibly terrify) you. If you think it might take 10-15 years to accomplish something, challenge yourself to think how you might begin to accomplish it right now.

6. Remember your Torch statement should fire you up and excite you. Long time frames are deadly, and often not achieved. It is passion more than time that will achieve your life dreams. So the issue is how to ignite that passion now before it wanes in the natural process of our graying and aging bodies.

7. Make the images from your goal exercises as concrete and imagistic as possible. Make them things you could "deliver" to yourself.

8. Paint the picture. Imagine the scenes that will bring your Torch to life. Imagine living in your dream, and fill in all its contours.

9. Construct your Torch statement: "If as a consequence of this work you were to deliver to yourself the following _____ how would that be?"

10. If you are not on fire, your Torch has likely not been lit.

11. If your Torch has not been fully lit, increase the offering, double the stakes, cut the time frame in half. Make it unbelievably exciting.

12. Let go of your doubts. Park them. We'll deal with them later. The biggest challenge for a self-help person at this stage is suspending your disbelief, particularly around your financial situation. A financial Life Planner will often be much clearer about what is possible to accomplish in your life and how your internalized money messages (see "Innocent Messages" in *Seven Stages of Money Maturity* (1999)) are holding you back.

13. Continue to paint the picture and live into the dream. Give yourself plenty of time to live in this space, for at least a day, preferably a couple of weeks, before you begin to address the obstacles. Make your dream richer and richer as you live into it. Make it alive. Your passion will change the world – this is the life you were meant to live and this is the person the world most needs you to be. It is your brilliance, your genius, your authenticity. It is what sets the world on fire.

Couples

We've used a number of examples thus far of couples being Life Planned, and even when there are dramatic differences between their individual Torches, we've seen how they come together. Truth is, couples are more likely to fall apart if they don't find a way to acknowledge and support the full realization of each other's Life Plan. A popular book on child rearing is entitled, *Whole Child, Whole Parent* (1997), by Polly Berrien Berrends. It is equally true, "whole partner, whole couple." Both partners need to focus first on fulfilling their own heart's core life. It is the principle of putting on your own oxygen mask first, and then turning to help those around you. This is why, in filling out the goal exercises, we ask that each spouse or each partner do their own work separately, and not share the work with each other until they come to our office for the Vision meeting.

There were many examples in my career of couples who seemed to fall in love again in my office as they revealed their answers to Heart's Core or Question Three, and I hear stories from Registered Life Planners® all the time along the same lines. I'd like to share a rather dramatic story I heard recently from an adviser on the west coast.

The story is a short one; she told it to me in brief. She had a middle income, or "middle market" client base, charged on an hourly basis, and often combined the Exploration and Vision meetings for her less well-to-do clients. A new couple had come to see her a few months earlier. They were in their late 40s but had a heaviness about them that made the Life Planner think they were a decade older. They hardly looked at each other during the early stages of the engagement. Each had an attitude of resignation, as if they had grown into the attitude mutually over time. What came out of the Exploration phase was that their 13-year-old only daughter had killed herself a dozen years ago, and they had been unable to find much purpose around anything since. They had come in to see the financial Life Planner around the usual mix of economic questions, but as they began to talk about their individual goals in Questions One and Two, the adviser was surprised at how they would begin to look at each other and say things like, "Wow, I didn't know you liked to do that!" or "I remember you saying how much you would like to do that when we first got together. It's wonderful to hear it again after all these years." And when each came to the Third Question, the major regret for each was the loss of their daughter.

It became clear that in the 12 intervening years they had hardly been able to talk about the loss with each other, rather staying in a place of despair, self-blame and deep regret. When I heard the story, I thought how amazing it was that the couple had even managed to stay together through all those years. But what was more amazing to me was how the Life Planner was able to put together in their Torch statement many of the old, long unspoken dreams that the couple had somehow held onto in the intervening years, along with a closing ceremony over a long weekend away at a favorite place dedicated to their daughter, with the focus on saying goodbye, forgiving and asking forgiveness, and on moving forward. Most amazing of all, perhaps, was that it worked!

Final Thoughts

At its most profound, Vision has nothing to do with seeing where we are going, who we will be, what we will do (Vision has nothing to do, for instance, with "vision statements" popular in corporate boardrooms), and everything to do with seeing into who we really are, seeing into how our buds will most naturally flower, how the fruit will ripen. Great Life Planners will see these things in us and support them, trained in listening skills to do both. They can only do it if they deserve our trust (that is part of the function of the Exploration meeting, earning our trust), and engage with us in a kind of vision quest that is the function of the Vision meeting.

Even if we don't use a Life Planner, our Life Plan is about seeing into our own nature and finding our natural rhythms. It is about discovering our passionate purpose and then designing our own way of delivering it into the world.

EVOKE® hinges on a moment in the Vision interview we call "Lighting the Torch." It is the moment we come alive. Without it there is no real Life Plan. Just a hodge-podge of goals, a data gatherer's delight but a Life Planner's nightmare. If you are using a financial adviser, watch out for planners relying more on their computer questionnaires than on their insight and their connection with you and your dreams. You need the Torch. How can you develop a Life Plan when you don't know what you're aiming to have or do or become? The Obstacles segment becomes impossible to navigate, a low-energy affair that gets murky or goes nowhere or that can take years, lost in internal spaces more suitable for a psychologist than a financial Life Planner.

I am reminded of William Blake's poem, *Jerusalem*, not his visionary 100-page magnum opus of illuminated text by the same name, but his short poem sung at every British football match and many a formal occasion, what the Brits call their "unofficial national anthem."

And did those feet in ancient time
Walk upon England's mountain green?
And was the holy Lamb of God
On England's pleasant pastures seen?
And did the countenance divine
Shine forth upon our clouded hills?
And was Jerusalem builded here
Among those dark satanic mills?

Bring me my bow of burning gold!
Bring me my arrows of desire!
Bring me my spear! O clouds, unfold!
Bring me my chariot of fire!
I will not cease from mental fight,
Nor shall my sword sleep in my hand,
Till we have built Jerusalem
In England's green and pleasant land.

Vision is where we receive our call to greatness, where we take up the hero's journey. We have come to our real sense of purpose, whether we get there on our own or with the help of someone who believes in us so much we find it unbelievable.

Vision is not always an easy place. Often it is a place of "mental fight" and it can be surrounded by Blake's "dark satanic mills" that threaten to crowd out the building of our true Jerusalem. Or sometimes it is with a touch of terror that we recognize that our family is more important than our job, that our values must come front and center amongst our economic choices, that our deepest dreams of creative action, of writing a book, playing music or creating an unusual company have been diminishing day by day and year by year, as if the dreams were indeed surrounded by sleep rather than visionary action. It is a place that often calls for our bows of burning gold, our chariots of fire.

So take the visions you have created for yourself in this chapter and make them sing. Paint the picture, brighter and brighter, rich in imagination, magnificent in texture.

We've been making a huge mistake individually and collectively as a society, politically, economically and personally. We've thought the money world is all about financial products, about Wall Street, credit cards, interest rates, wages, savings and debt. Or it's about bargains, opportunities, deals that we negotiate to navigate our world.

But the truth is, money is all about us and access to ourselves – our passions, our sacred purposes, "our countenance divine." An unhealthy relationship with money robs us of these things. We can complain about the government, corporations, unions, international organizations and get nowhere – or we can identify our passionate purposes and begin to change the world – at the very least our world – by putting the financial architecture in place to make our visions happen. That's what Vision is all about – identifying our passionate purposes so that we can bring them right to the center of all of our life, our economic life as well, and change the world at last by making them happen.

Making them happen is the business of the rest of this book.

Obstacles - EVOKE®
Bringing Vitality to Everything You Do

The Obstacles stage in EVOKE® is in many ways the most exciting of all the stages. It's where things really begin to happen. It's where all those excuses we had for being stuck, all our apologies, doubts and regrets not only fade away but are actually transformed into action – and action upon action on exactly the things we care about the most. You've seen how Exploration is the place where we finally put all our cards on the table, and Vision is where our Torch is lit and becomes clear. Well, Obstacles is where that Torch both illuminates and burns into the world exactly the pathways necessary to bring our genius to light and allow our authenticity to flourish in everything we do. The process has a natural development to it. The brighter the Torch, the clearer the challenges and obstacles. But with a Torch so bright, nothing can stand in its way. It energizes us into action. Let's look at some examples of the challenges the Obstacles phase presents and how they are resolved.

Painting the Picture

The Hawaiian preacher is a good place to start. Recall that at first Roger tried to deny his dream. Later he tried to convince us both that it would be impossible to accomplish. And, of course, he was right about certain aspects of that impossible dream. Those aspects were what kept him from even contemplating accomplishing it in the first place. He knew he didn't have the skills, the resources or the temperament to permanently leave his work and to live in the jungle, as much as he would love to sabbatical and meditate there. By making the dream both larger than he could accomplish and larger than what he really wanted, it was easy for him to reject the dream and let discouragement and exhaustion instead become embedded in his life in the place where his passion and his spirit should have thrived.

I'm afraid this has been true for many of us. Clearly a lot of Roger's obstacles were inner, among them denial, doubt and lethargy. But as we clarified what the dream was that would really excite him about his life, giving him the promise and the hope of dedicating three months a year to spiritual work and living in the heart of the jungle that surrounded him, the lethargy and denial were almost immediately replaced by a river of energy driving toward the task of resolving his remaining inner obstacle of doubt and his two overarching external obstacles of finances and the politics of expectation within his church community.

It turned out the finances were not as challenging as he thought. His life in the jungle would be simple and not require much. His main concern was covering a variety of monthly expenses while he was gone. He figured that if he could find the right replacement for his services, that person could cover many of those expenses. And his doubt diminished daily against his excitement and the steady crafting, with the aid of local friends, of the details of where and how his jungle retreat would take place.

What remained was the most challenging obstacle of all, the steady and seemingly obstinate refusal of the leadership in his congregation to go along. With a good heart, Roger tried everything, wooing the stewards of the community individually and collectively, but nothing worked. Finally, in a more heated session with the leadership, he realized what was wrong. Sure, there was some lethargy and despondency in the congregation from feeling abandoned by Roger, but how that played out was an unwillingness to search for, engage and structure the visiting preachers' time, expectations and responsibilities. So Roger leapt to work, advertising through his worldwide denomination for pastors who would like to spend a summer in Hawaii. He drafted responsibilities, salary structures, set up how they could live in his space and pay his bills. He made the transition so simple and easy his congregation had to say yes. And he made the experiences for the visitors so enjoyable they would often try to return for a second and third year.

There are many things to learn from the pastor's experience. One is to see how powerful a positive passion is, how much clarity and then vigor it can provide for us, seemingly out of nowhere. Another is the value of listing clearly all the obstacles we can think of, including inner obstacles. In order to do that we need the clearest of possible Torches. Only with such clarity will each obstacle and its solution become obvious to us.

"How much is enough?" is a question often asked by people about money. It is the centerpiece of Lee Eisenberg's marvellous book on money, *The Number* (2006). We might view the question of enough as the clarification of our dream. It is a critical question for our Torch. Somewhere between the lighting of the Torch toward the end of the Vision meeting, and the first ten minutes or so of the Obstacles meeting, we engage in the process we call "painting the picture," where we make the vision as clear as we can possibly imagine it. One of the things that happens in that process is, with our seemingly "impossible dreams," we find just the balance that fully energizes and excites us about our life and our Life Plan. If we compromise too much back to "reality," the Life Planning process really doesn't do anything for us, our life continues along as hum drum as it has always been. On the other hand, if we give ourselves fulltime the life in the cabin in the jungle, we might face an uncertain future, lose the community we love so much and the capacity to make a difference in their lives and find ourselves as much in despair once again as we already are. But finding the right balance, in this case finding a way to live in the jungle three months out of every year, energizes every aspect of our lives.

We often face the twin dangers of not being daring enough, and thus living a diminished life – and daring too much, beyond our economic means or our true comfort zone and jeopardizing our future and other important areas of our lives. In Life Planning we discover that most people have dared too little, and too often ignored the things that they really care about the most. We also discover that often these things won't break the bank, won't take that much economically to deliver, and will bless us with enormous reserves of newfound energy that we will be able to apply to every area of our lives, including economic. More often than not, we've found that releasing these most profound passions brings the person alive, and economic issues become easier rather than harder as a consequence.

Timothy is an example. When he realized he could have his dream of sailing round the world, everything changed for him. When he and Mary walked into my office two weeks later he took me by surprise. The first words out of his mouth were "I've got the boat, George," and he continued.

"Yeah, I was so energized at the end of our meeting last time, I didn't know what to do with it. So I got on the phone when I got home and started calling all of my sailing buddies to see what they thought, to see if they had any ideas how I could make it happen. I think it was the third or fourth person who said, 'Why don't you see if one of your friends will rent you the boat or lend it to you?' I just kept calling. It was actually a lot of fun. I got lots of ideas for the trip. I think it was the tenth person I talked with who made it happen. I couldn't quite believe it, so I called two more people after that. Anyway, the fellow's wife had been diagnosed with cancer and he'd been feeling his age as well. 'It's what I always dreamed of,' he said. 'I don't figure I'll be doing it now, but it would give me the greatest pleasure to think that you were doing it in my stead and in my boat.' We both choked up at that." Timothy paused, lump in his throat.

A few minutes later he told me another shift that had occurred. He had changed his mind around work. He'd talked to his friend with the boat about it and he decided not to sail right away, but to put it off for twelve months. Over the course of that time I watched him as he poured himself into his work.

What he had found depressing, he now found energizing. As I mentioned, I felt they were close to having enough already for a modest retirement. He figured devoting an extra year to work, he could save that much more and experiment cutting expenses at the same time. What he hadn't counted on was his boss noticing – so much so that at the end of that 12 months Timothy figured he could have a part-time job if he wanted on his return. Unnecessary if he decided to sail on or to retire, but nice to think of as a safety net in any case.

The most surprising thing about their economic situation that came out of our work was that Mary's shop had become strong enough as a business to have real sale value. Moreover, as they came to terms with Timothy's sailing, they offered a room in the house to a niece for the summer along with an internship in Mary's business. The niece was finishing a college degree in biology, considering an MBA and was fascinated with Mary's business. A responsible worker, she made it easier for Mary to follow Timothy a couple of times that summer, but also gave Mary the opportunity to consider how she might expand her success and build an even stronger business.

When our vision is passionate and strong, obstacles energize us and seemingly resolve themselves in the face of our vitality.

In the cases of Roger, Timothy and Mary, nearly all of the obstacles and their solutions were identified and resolved by the profound interest and passion of the clients themselves. All that was necessary for me to do was facilitate the discussion with my own enthusiasm for their Torches and my seasoned optimism that where there was a will, we would find the way.

Louis with Ben and Anita

When Ben and Anita came in for their third meeting, Ben was on fire. Louis hardly needed to ask his usual, "Has anything changed since our last meeting?"

Ben said for the first time since he left his old job, he'd been thinking about his opportunities rather than his disappointments. He'd begun to design his new business, begun research on specific legislation for exporting food and wine to China, and begun to talk with potential vendors and partners in the operation.

He'd been dreaming as well, looking at the change in lifestyle that might come with all of this and shared those dreams with Anita. At the same time, he'd been looking at opportunities to earn current income.

"One of my former competitors asked whether I would like to work for him," Ben blurted out, looking a little sheepish.

"Wow," Louis said.

"I feel torn," Ben said.

"Hm."

"It's not the work that's a problem but the thought of a boss pushing me around again," Ben said. "It's the lack of freedom. Frankly I don't really want the job, but both Anita and I would feel much more comfortable as we move forward with our businesses, if there was income available, and we weren't just spending down our assets. I think we would have much more energy for our new ideas."

"Ah," Louis said.

Pause.

"Can you see any way to do the same work in another setting, one that has freedom for you?" Louis asked.

Ben paused.

"Well actually, yes," he said. "I think I do." He explained how one of his former colleagues hired himself out as an interim manager. "They aren't weighed down by the history of their work there, nor by attachment to a long-term job. Instead they can set specific goals and go at them," Ben said.

"Do you think the company that has reached out to you would hire you as an interim?" Louis asked.

"I'm not sure," Ben said. "But others might."

Pause.

"I just realized that this means I don't have to work a normal work week."

"Wow," Louis responded.

"Maybe I could work four days a week as an interim manager and spend the other day on my trade business. When that starts to make money, I can cut back again on the interim management."

Louis could see that for Ben the prospect of more freedom and less stress filled him with vigor. In fact Ben was re-lighting his own Torch here, moving from despondency around work to excitement again around newfound freedom.

"Ben, this seems so doable to me, what on earth could keep you from realizing this?"

"But what if I can't find a position as interim manager?

"OK, let's look at that, and is there anything else that stands in your way?" Louis asked.

Ben didn't answer Louis' question but began to solve his own. "Louis, I have an idea of which companies to approach and how to approach them."

Ben was both energized and excited by these new ideas, and shortly he changed the subject and began to talk about the trade business. Louis noticed that clearly this was where his real passion lay, and that it wasn't diminished one iota by the prospect of a four day a week job.

"I'll write a business plan for our next meeting, Louis. I can't see anything that will get in the way."

Louis smiled. "Not with the passion you have for it, Ben! Would it be alright if I worked with Anita now?"

Anita was clearly pleased at the energy of her husband, had had productive conversations herself regarding her new business during the intervening weeks, but deflected Louis' attempts to discuss them with her, saying over and over again how relieved they would be if Ben got a job. At one point she revealed that she was concerned about her new business partner in her venture. Louis reminded her of her Torch at that moment, how much it meant to her, what an extraordinary difference it would make in her life if she achieved it. As she listened to him articulating exactly the possibilities that excited her most, she regained her energy, and when he asked, "What could possibly get in the way of that?" with only the slightest hesitation she said "Nothing. Nothing at all."

Then Anita shared how she had called an old friend and discussed the possibility of a business partnership.

"My friend was quite interested and has a good business sense," she said. "But a potential problem is that I don't want to do this every day. Plus, I'm not sure if my new business partner has the same dedication as I do to the idea. Or if we will match each other," Anita said.

As Louis reminded her again of her Torch, Anita came up with solutions that pleased her to each obstacle that arose. She recognized that she could do the work part-time, just as Ben was doing with his China business, and she got excited as she listed the very different skills that Carlo, her business partner, would bring to the business. She became eager for the next conversation with him outlining in greater detail their different roles and responsibilities.

Anita promised that she too would write a business plan prior to the next meeting.

With this, Louis knew they were both on solid ground and he felt certain they could execute on their plans. Each Torch was brightly lit and they were confident and motivated to find solutions to the obstacles themselves. They made a new appointment three weeks later to look at the work they intended to do and to evaluate the progress.

As you've perhaps guessed, the most important moment in an Obstacles meeting typically comes with the relighting of the Torch. It is a critical moment because if the Torch is not blazing, you can't be sure what the vision really is, and if you don't know what you're aiming at, how can you possibly know what the obstacles to it are. This lack of clarity is the situation that many financial advisers and their clients find themselves in. It's an unfortunate one, and explains in part why most people who need a financial planner don't work with one, prefer to do it themselves, and why those who have a financial adviser aren't tremendously keen on the process.

If the vision isn't articulated in a way that sets the client on fire, client and adviser have two choices. Either they go forward with a muted goal, or they focus simply on the financials, hardly an inspiring situation for the consumer, although it pays the adviser's fees and makes him feel important. In the past the focus on the financials has led to the products the "adviser" wants to sell, driving trust in the adviser and the whole "advice" system about as low as it could go in a consumer's eyes. But even if the focus on the financials is not product-centered, even if it is genuine advice, if it lacks an inspiring goal, it's like being in the dentist's office, an experience you think is good for you, but are eager to get over.

Financial work should have tremendous meaning to each of us, because it is the work that helps us articulate what we are most passionate about, and then it is the work that puts the financial architecture in place for us to become the people we truly want to be. A financial adviser's office should be an inspiring place to be, because it is the place where we see most clearly our own most inspiring visions and how they will be realized.

If, on the other hand, we find ourselves focusing on a muted goal (or one from a financial planning textbook) we will lack all the vitality necessary for the work at hand, because there's neither clarity nor passion about why we're there. If the focus goes to the obstacles in the hope that clearing them away will reveal the vision that is lacking, unfortunately you will find that the obstacles are murky and unclear and very difficult to dispel. I mean, obstacles to what? We find ourselves searching in all the areas where we don't function at 100%, and all of those obstacles feel overwhelming and most likely are. If they are external they will involve drudge work we are not excited about, and if they are internal, it seems like years of psychotherapy couldn't remove them.

On the other hand, once we are passionate about our goals, all the work leading up to their accomplishment feels invigorating, many external obstacles turn out to be irrelevant or minor, and internal obstacles hardly present themselves to us at all. So if your Torch isn't blazing, don't bother with this chapter, go back to Vision and keep working on it by yourself or with a Life Planner until your Torch for living is blazing bright. Then, dive into the obstacles. You will find them easy to solve. In fact, one of the skills Life Planners learn is, whenever the obstacles seem to get too thick and challenging for a client, it's time to relight the Torch, to remind the client how marvellous and compelling their dream is, how important it is for them to achieve it, and how their vision will bring them exactly to the sense of accomplishment and purpose they have always longed to feel. Louis did this quite elegantly with Anita when she became discouraged and too dependent on Ben.

One of the reasons Life Planners are successful in their work is that they give so much of it over to their clients. For instance they realize it is their client, not the planner, who has most of the solutions to the Life Plan. After all it's their life, not the adviser's, in question. So you see Louis asking Ben and Anita what *their* solutions might look like. He has ideas of his own to help keep the meeting alive and vital, but Louis' *belief in his clients' dreams* is more important to Ben and Anita than his *ideas about their lives*. The planner's belief gives clients encouragement and the energy to solve the problems themselves. Before asking them what the solutions might be, the planner asks them what possibly could get in the way of their great objectives. The planner gets them to list all the obstacles they can think of before venturing forth with any he or she might see. Many is the time a skilled Life Planner will contribute little in the way of either obstacles or solutions, little that the client wasn't already aware of. But it's the planner's optimism, support and enthusiasm that keeps the client from collapsing into the impossibilities of their dream and burying it once again from light of day.

The trick in doing Life Planning for ourselves is to bring the same quality of confidence, excitement and appreciation to ourselves and our Torches as a Life Planner would. Without the encouragement of someone other than ourselves, the greatest resource we have is the inspiration of the Torch itself. Read it again and again. Write about it, elaborating upon it in every conceivable way, painting as vivid a picture as you can, until it becomes something you have no choice but to walk into, obstacles falling from you like water off a duck's back.

Peggy Frye is a Registered Life Planner® who worked at Citibank for 28 years, mostly in private banking. She once told me that the EVOKE® training gave her more confidence and understanding of how to work with clients than her entire prior 28 years of trainings at Citi. Recently she shared with me this inspiring story of her Obstacles work with a well-to-do client couple:

Mary and Will were matriarch and patriarch of an enormously talented family. Inspired by the Life Planning process, they had recently moved from a suburban home into the center of urban life. But they wanted to make significant changes and lead by example for their four adult children and spouses. In addition to their Life Plan, they offered the gift of Life Planning to each child and spouse who wanted to experience Life Planning as well.

Mary was instantly clear on her vision and truly excited about her Torch. She wanted to experience the beauty of the arts daily and to live all that the city had to offer. She also wanted more time with her grandchildren. Her Torch was clear and concise, and she was implementing almost before Peggy finished the Vision meeting.

Will on the other hand had had trouble even listing all of his answers to the Three Questions. He had always held his dreams and goals close to the vest, and Life Planning was truly a new experience. With some very thoughtful discussion, he was able to envision a life he would enjoy. He wanted to learn new languages and travel with his wife and grandchildren to places where he could speak those languages. He wanted their new urban townhouse to be a magnet for family gatherings. He wanted time to attend concerts with Mary, take long walks, and enjoy the hum of the city. He became quite excited as he described this.

In the Obstacles meeting, Peggy re-lit the Torch for Will, and then asked, "What could possibly keep you from this now that you are retired and living in the city?"

There was a long pause. "I have trouble finding the time," he said. She asked if there was anything else and as he elaborated his weekly responsibilities she could see he was getting quite angry. "I have very little time for me. I am retired, and I have so much to manage – the punch list on the new townhouse, litigation regarding the general contractor, a house and another apartment to prepare for sale and to manage, paying bills… I'm so frustrated and fed up with it all, I actually took a one-day anger management workshop last week. The instructor taught me how to meditate, but it's just another item on my to-do list. Now it's making me angry too!"

Again and again Peggy found herself re-lighting Will's Torch and reminding him of the great vision he had for his retired life. At the end of the meeting, Will had two simple pieces of homework. The first was to find time in his schedule for himself and the things he enjoyed. During that time he was to elaborate upon his vision of his ideal life. The second was to offload as many duties as possible. Peggy felt that she was opening his mind to new possibilities, but they really had not yet arrived at the way to overcome his obstacles.

The afternoon after the meeting, Peggy pondered how to help Will. She went back to a technique from her old banking days when she had a complex real estate transaction, and needed what they called a "spider gram" drawing to understand the deal. Peggy drew a spider gram for Will with him in the center and all his responsibilities emanating from the middle of the circle. The page was full of managing properties, preparing them for sale, dealing with realtors, paying all the bills. There was the management of a complicated chart of accounts for bills and legal entities on Quicken. There were general partnership duties. The list went on and on. It covered the entire page in small print. He was doing four jobs in retirement! He really did not have time for his life. No wonder he was angry – like an over-worked and under-paid employee who was being asked to do more.

They quickly met again. Peggy came armed with her hand-written spider gram. Both Will and Mary were amazed at the picture it painted. In fact, they added more jobs onto the picture that Peggy hadn't known about. Then, together, they went through each line, and brainstormed how to accomplish these jobs in another way. What can we find for others to do? How can we manage the process of off-loading and yet trust that it is done correctly? The implementation plan was underway. They categorized his duties into Fun To Do jobs (he did love some of them), Ought To Do jobs (the ones most critical to outsource), and Heart's Core jobs, ones that inspired him as much as traveling, family and learning new languages. Mary and Will left that day with concrete steps to overcome the obstacles.

They spent several months using the hand-written spider gram to steadily diminish the obstacles to Will's new life. Peggy says at last Will has been loving his life in the city, learning new languages and just came back from a trip to Paris with Mary and his grandchildren.

As you might gather from these examples, there are specific stages to an Obstacle meeting, and in particular to solving the obstacles to a particular part of our vision. It starts with the Torch. It moves to a "painted picture." Then all the obstacles we can think of are listed and put on the table. Then, for one obstacle at a time, we come up with one, two, three, a dozen possible solutions until we are clear about how we will solve this problem and we feel energized and excited. Let's look at an example that happens every week in a Life Planner's office, and that happened over and over again for my clients over the course of my career.

A couple comes into a Life Planner's office. They have individual goals, exciting to each of them, but one of the core goals they share in common. They would each like to spend more time with each other and with their children. Let's say the father is working full-time, the mother part-time. She is feeling conflicted about her work, partly just wanting to be a mom, partly keeping on with her career. Both realize how rapidly the children are growing up, how fleeting and precious each moment is to be with them. As a family, they have limited economic flexibility.

Among the solutions that I have seen discussed or implemented that free up either time or money:

- Selling the family home, capturing its equity, and moving to a less expensive part of the country.

- Moving to a less expensive part of the city.

- Tapping into the home equity with a loan.

- Dropping television time in the evening, and substituting engaged time with the children instead.

- Dropping golf and other private time on the weekends to spend more time with the family, or bringing the family onto the links.

- Taking a year or two off to just be with the family, or to travel inexpensively together.

- Taking music lessons together, and playing music together in the evening.

- Playing games together each evening.

- Leaving work earlier every day of the week, or just one day a week.

- Working a "normal" work week instead of lots of unpaid overtime.

- Working from home more, and using the travel time saved to be with the family.

- Shifting from an employee status to being self-employed to be able to spend more time at home.

- Finding efficiencies at work to capture more time.

- Finding ways to charge more or earn more for your work.

- Listing all of the things that each family member most wants to do with the others, and then making them all happen.

- Cutting down on expenses and substituting more family events.

- Designing wildly creative holidays for the family.

- Designing creative evenings and weekends.

- Spending more one on one time with each child.

- Coaching their children's sports and other events.

I'm sure I've left out far more solutions here than I have listed. Coming up with them, and playing creatively is one of the joys of the Obstacles phase of EVOKE®. Clearly some of these solutions have economic consequences. Others don't. Often where the economics look challenging, as the couple move towards a new lifestyle more in keeping with their values, new economic opportunities and understandings arise that make their financial situation easier rather than harder.

As you might recall, Gabri Verbeek, from the Netherlands, owned a thriving insurance business with 17 employees. He lost it all, practically overnight, and went bankrupt. For several years, as he developed his new profession of Registered Life Planner®, he inspired me (and others) with stories of how he and his family coped. They lost their cars, they lost their home, they lost everything except the love they had for each other. We think we are always doing our children a favor when we earn money to pay family bills, but one day as Gabri was contemplating a job for very low wages and long hours that he wouldn't enjoy, one of his four children came up to him and said, "Daddy, I'd rather see you at home and have time with you. I can live with one pair of jeans, holes and all, but I don't want to miss you every day. I want to see you here!" Gabri figured out how to work while his children were at school, and develop his home-based, self-employed Life Planner practice, so that he could dedicate more time to his children.

Gabri has been an inspiration to many of us in the Life Planning movement, showing us how we can live true to our values and our Life Plans on very little. Nonetheless it is a common refrain, particularly from those trying to do it themselves on meager means: "If you're not rich, how can you do this?" "What if you're in debt?" "How do I live my Life Plan on a budget?"

I've seen my clients do many things, and have done many myself. Among the seemingly infinite solutions I've seen (a few of which we elaborate upon in Knowledge):

- Get rid of your car – use a bicycle or walk; or use a service such as Zipcar; carpool
- Buy a used car instead of new; drive fuel efficient cars
- Grow your own food; cook at home; make lunches; minimize fast food and restaurant meals
- Work well for your employer and then negotiate a raise and/or more flex time
- Get paid more for night shift or weekend shift
- Scale back everything, minimize costs while working at the highest paying job you can find for a few years, saving like crazy in order to fund a more flexible life thereafter
- Make a budget, economize on everything – both practical things and more fun things; master the art of simplified living
- Payoff debt and then continue to save at the same rate, building economic flexibility
- Save all your receipts and review monthly to see where money is spent and look for places to economize
- Take advantage of all tax deductions, especially if self-employed
- Hire others to do a task as well as you or better, if you can earn more money by working more instead
- Rent movies and watch at home instead of going to the theater
- Give up cable TV, use the computer instead
- Use the library and used bookstores, used CD's and used movies
- Reduce bills by comparing insurance rates, calling utilities to ask if you're getting the lowest rate. Raise deductibles.

- Rent rooms/space in your home
- Shop for clothing/furniture at consignment/used clothing and furniture stores, garage sales
- Swap child care with other families as well as toys, clothing for children
- Find free leisure time activities such as hiking, biking, skating, etc; free museum days, street fairs.
- Use coupon services such as "Groupon" for savings on activities and restaurants; use reward sites to accumulate points for merchandise; take advantage of rewards programs at retailers
- Extreme couponing – search online for coupons to cover most grocery purchases
- Shop at big box stores, buy in bulk; buy store brands; don't buy bottled water
- Barter for services; share tools, lawn equipment with neighbors
- Shop on Amazon or eBay for lower cost products
- Make own cleaning supplies, cosmetics, beer/wine, etc.
- Get debt counseling; restructure your debt
- Declare bankruptcy
- It's important to both economize and live your Life Plan:
- If you're self-employed – work overtime for six months then part-time for six months
- Restructure your work, so time for creativity, spirit, entrepreneurial endeavors and family life is not compromised
- Work no overtime at all
- Take advantage of all vacation and medical time
- Do 40 hours work in three or four days and take long weekends
- Combine work and pleasure, work and family

- Match vacation time and weekend time to your Life Plan and passionate purposes

- Find a job you love instead of one you hate

- Seek out a fee-only financial adviser who specializes in helping those who aren't rich.

Remember Jennifer, the young woman with significant college debt who wanted a career that combined fitness and nursing? Bryan Gasparro, the RLP®️ she worked with, advised her to use her father's financial gift to pay down her debt rather than for the purchase of a home. She landed a job as a nurse at a dance academy, satisfying her goal of working as a health professional in a fitness environment. She took on a roommate to split rent, food and other costs and directed 12% of her income toward her loans. Watching the principal balance decrease on her monthly statements was liberating, she reported to Bryan a year after their first meeting. In the evenings and on weekends, she worked as a personal trainer for considerably more per hour than her day job in order to fund travel and start a savings account for a future home, two items at the forefront of her Questions One and Two. Although her personal time was diminished, the satisfaction she gained from her work, along with the financial rewards, more than made up for what she viewed as the temporary loss of free time. She believed her relaxed attitude and new found freedom facilitated her meeting "a great guy" at the gym, a fitness enthusiast and medical professional as well.

Inner Obstacles

Sometimes it's the external obstacles alone that need to be addressed, but often we can address a single internal obstacle and suddenly everything becomes straightforward. Recall how powerfully the Hawaiian preacher's actions and excitement became when he overcame lethargy and denial, simply by painting a very clear picture of what it was that he wanted. Sometimes the Torch itself is simply a collection of inner goals. One such goal that a young pastor shared with me last year: "I want to live with freshness in each moment as if the moment were alive. I want to act with authenticity in everything I do." The following inner goals have all appeared prominently in Third Questions and Heart's Core columns over the years:

Inner Goals

Simplicity	Compassion	Meditation	God-consciousness
Kindness	Clear-thinking	Spirit	Acceptance
Honesty	Calmness	Ease	Forgiveness
Patience	Equanimity	Generosity	Vitality
Authenticity	Energy	Aloha	Vigor
Love	Prayer	Ethical understanding	Presence

You might think that neither the solutions nor the obstacles to internal goals can possibly be financial, and that the goals themselves have no place in a financial adviser's office, but often where these goals are part of the person's passionate purpose, they require time and real attention. Taking the time to address them will often, but not always, require financial resources or financial sacrifices. In addition, financial excuses are often the predominant blocks to developing or achieving these extraordinary human qualities. What a shame! And how inappropriate that we have banished these conversations from the world of finance. With the advent of Life Planning, that will happen no longer.

So What are the Obstacles to the Inner Goals, and What are the Inner Obstacles to Any Kind of Goal, and What are the Solutions to Inner Obstacles?

Here are some of the external obstacles we see to the development of inner goals:

- Don't have the time

- Don't have the money

- Don't have a clue how to do it

- Don't know who can help

- Don't know of communities of learning or support

- Never done contemplative or meditative exercises

- My spouse can't relate

- My friends can't relate

- Don't have a methodology for change

Some of the internal obstacles to any goal include:

- Lethargy
- Frustration
- Impatience
- Boredom
- Habitual responses
- Anger
- Anxiety
- Depression
- Shame
- Guilt
- Restlessness
- Doubt
- Uncertainty
- Resistance
- Addictive behavior
- Dependencies

If some of these obstacles are getting in your way, you might look at *Transforming Suffering into Wisdom* (2010). It is full of exercises and practices, both internal and external, to make our accumulation of virtues and living our values an ever increasing dedication and an integral part of our daily life. I have also seen the most wonderful solutions come from client sessions, and from advisers I've trained all over the world. Among the most successful solutions are the following:

- Simple daily affirmations
- Making commitments to change
- Finding a mentor, therapist, spiritual counselor or coach

- Reading James O. Prochaska's *Changing for Good* (1995) and embedding its practices for changing troublesome habits into your daily life.

- Daily re-dedication to your passionate purposes, your Torch

- Living the Third Question

- Joining groups dedicated to similar tasks

- Joining spiritual, church or values-based communities

- Joining web-based communities

- Reading books dedicated to your task

- Accumulating wisdom sayings and practicing their wisdom

- Keeping a journal

Self-Help

At the end of the Obstacles phase of EVOKE®, we are energized and invigorated by the actions we've begun to take and by the transformations in our thinking and our commitments to our deeper purposes. Many elements of our plan have become clear, and we are ready for the next meeting where the full design of the plan will be revealed, including how the finances will work. Let's look now at specific steps we might take if we were to do Obstacles ourselves, without a Life Planner's assistance, how we might approach and overcome the obstacles.

1. Your first step is to write out the Torch from your Vision work with as much detail as possible. What we call, "painting the picture." Make it as vivid, exciting and fresh to your senses as possible. As if you were actually there as it becomes realized. Wherever you see the opportunity, add locations, imagine where you will be standing or sitting or walking. Put in the people who will be with you or nearby. Imagine times of year, different weather. Show the enjoyment you will have. Make your dream alive! Fully live into the freedom you have created in your mind. I encourage you to do

your Obstacles work on the website (www.lifeplanningforyou.com) as you have with Exploration and Vision.

2. Once you feel complete and fulfilled in the painted picture, the second step is to list every external obstacle you can think of to the accomplishment of your vision. Your list might include financial obstacles, time constraints, as well as people who might object or whose assistance you need. There might be place issues as well: where will you accomplish the work, for instance? Everything you can think of.

3. The third step is to list every internal obstacle you can think of. For instance, it might be that gaining a PhD in computer science requires perseverance and overcoming doubt, whereas being a better parent might call for greater patience or empathy. Or perhaps it's kindness and patience themselves you've listed in your Torch as qualities you want to develop, and your inner obstacles include stubbornness, irascibility, a quickness to judgment.

4. Periodically throughout this exercise, if you feel overwhelmed by your obstacles and find yourself losing the energy you found with the Torch, it is time to relight the Torch for yourself. Go back to your painted picture. Remind yourself how long you have held back from its delivery, and how crucial it is that you live into this vision of yourself. Remember that it contains the promise of bringing you freedom for the fulfilment of your deepest, truest, best self. Stay with this vision until you really connect with it, you live it and you find the passion and the fire inside yourself again. Then when it's really blazing come back to the obstacles you must overcome. Remind yourself also that you don't need to overcome all the obstacles by yourself, that if you need help, you will be able to reach out and find others who will support you in your dream.

5. Next to the list of obstacles, inner and outer, list their solutions, multiple solutions to some of them, all that you can think of, how you will solve them. If you get stumped by any of them, remind yourself again of your Torch, and list those whom you will ask for help around a particular obstacle. Keep going until you have

an active approach to each obstacle and feel optimistic and excited about achieving your goals.

6. In a similar process, now list your other goals, particularly the ones that feel critical (and critical economically), but were not necessarily in your Torch. These might include retirement, education for your children, funding a new home or vacations, providing for your loved ones if you were to pass away, and any number of other goals.

7. Continue to list the obstacles and solutions to these goals as well. If you ever feel your Torch diminishing, let go of the obstacles for now and return to your vision. Live in it for as long as is necessary to feel on fire and unshakable in your commitments. You might need several days or weeks with this at times. Take the time you need. This is your legacy; this is what you are on earth to do. Don't let anything hold you back. Then return to the obstacles, or to finding the people who can support and help make your vision real.

Concluding Exercises and Preparation for Knowledge

Two tasks remain in Obstacles to prepare you for the financial planning process in Knowledge, the next phase of EVOKE®, which will be the subject of the next chapter:

1. Gathering financial data and questions.

2. Identifying the time and money requirements for your more values-based goals.

Gathering Financial Data and Questions

It is useful in Obstacles, to gather all the materials you will need in Knowledge. Gathering together your financial data may well uncover more Obstacles, which will be useful to see at this stage, but may feel overwhelming to confront. Once again, if you start to feel the spark of vigor dimming in you, simply return to your Torch and relight it so that it is burning brightly. Deepen once again into the vision of your life that you are about to step into, and paint that picture in vivid detail in your mind. Trust in the process ahead to get you there. Be sure to note the obstacles, questions and concerns that arise as you pull out your insurance papers, bank statements, budgets or house documents so that they can be fully addressed and resolved in the Knowledge phase. The finances are meant merely to provide the architecture, the bricks and mortar to sustain your vision throughout your life. You must live into your dream. That is number one. Let your excitement and vitality from that dream add vigor to addressing your financial requirements so that you supply to your life what is necessary for it to thrive. The questions that arise are both natural and valuable. Their resolution takes place beginning in Obstacles, and then more fully in Knowledge, and finally in Execution.

Identifying the Time and Money Constraints and Freedoms That Will Arise From Accomplishing Your Goals

You have already begun the Knowledge phase of EVOKE® while still in Obstacles, as you are beginning to put your plan in place, and also begun Execution and the accomplishment of your plan as you immediately implement the first steps. Some of the aspects of Knowledge and Execution are about realizing very personal dreams, including things like "being authentic in all that I do" or "playing jazz in clubs once a week." As we've mentioned, often such seemingly immaterial and personal goals require time, and time may have to be taken from moneymaking occupations. We've also noted that often what we lose in time we gain in vitality, vigor and efficiency. So it is not unusual for what we perceive as a time drain to give us back as much or more in time than what we have lost. And when you consider that what the achievement of our goals is really giving us is the freedom we've always longed for in our lives to fulfil our callings and dreams, and that freedom is felt throughout all of our life activities, it is an amazing deal we are getting—far greater gain than cost!

Still, it is useful, as we head to the Knowledge phase of EVOKE® actually to measure and account for the changes that we are accomplishing or anticipating so we fully understand the impact they will have on our daily lives.

So you might fill out a chart like this to track the gains and losses of time and money as you go forward through Obstacles and beyond. Most of you will be surprised at how much more productive you become as you allow yourself to live your Life Plan.

Goal	Time it Will Take	Cost	Where Does Time Come From? Amounts		How Much Time Will You Gain At Work From		Money Gain/Loss
			Other Personal Activities	Money-Making Activities	Efficiencies	Profitable Energy	

Concluding Thoughts

I sometimes see Obstacles as a visionary space, and a space of enormous vitality and transformation. This is the progression we normally see.

A Vision → *An Obstacle* → *A Solution* → *then Dozens of Solutions.*
A Vision of the life worth living is grasped and energizes us.
An Obstacle arises casting a temporary cloud of doubt on our dream.
A Solution arises, lifting much of the doubt.

Then in rapid succession a dozen solutions appear, overlapping each other and adding new excitement and energy to the vision whose painted picture becomes suddenly brighter and clearer than ever before.

In Obstacles we strengthen our dreams, so much so that it is clear for us what needs to happen in Knowledge. For a Life Planner, the financial plan is so much easier than for a traditional financial planner, because the client's vision is crystal clear. If we are doing our financial plan ourselves without an adviser, this is even more the case. Think about it. No wonder finances can bore or overwhelm us, adding layers of anxiety to much that we do. What is the point of investing, saving, retirement programs, budgets, if we do not have a clear vision of what we want to accomplish with them? On the other hand, finances can be thrilling if we understand how they are helping us get where we long to go. And with the confidence that comes in the Obstacles phase that we see that we can actually accomplish those "impossible dreams" that will bring great meaning to our lives, we suddenly can see the purposes of money and put energy into harnessing its power as never before.

So now that you've become clear on what your purposes are, it's time to move to the Knowledge phase of EVOKE®, and design the financial plan that will accomplish the rest of your life's dream.

Knowledge - EVO**K**E®
Putting the Plan in Place

In Knowledge we use money skills to deliver our Life Plan in the most efficient and secure of possible ways. In a financial Life Planner's office, Knowledge is when the financial plan and various financial analyses are presented as well as the plan for action on life and financial goals. Throughout the first three phases of EVOKE®, Exploration, Vision and Obstacles, part of each meeting has been dedicated to gathering the financial information that helps facilitate Life Planning. Now it's time to put it all together, finances and life.

Without a plan of action, with time frames and accountability for those actions, many of us will slide back into the easy lethargy of our everyday lives. This is the huge benefit of the Knowledge phase of EVOKE®, particularly with financial matters that tend to bore or overwhelm us. As you read through this chapter, it would be particularly useful to visit the companion website, www.lifeplanningforyou.com, to complete the various net worth, budget and cash flow exercises critical to addressing the Knowledge items needed to accomplish your Life Plan.

Once the Obstacles phase is complete, we are motivated, like never before, to bring our Life Plan to fruition and quickly. We may have been blocked around the money side of our life in the past, but no longer. We have all the motivation we need to save money, to save time, to make money, and to avoid costly mistakes and unforeseen disasters. We have a willingness to learn financial skills that we've never had before, or to seek out the financial professionals who can help us.

Knowledge is where the Life Plan becomes a financial Life Plan. Here are some of the ways financial Knowledge benefits your Life Plan:

- *Budgets, cash flow, net worth statements and projections* help you save, get out of debt, and time your progress and the accomplishment of your Life Plan.

- *Savings and investment accounts, stocks, bonds, commodities and money markets* help you make money more quickly and efficiently toward the delivery of your Life Plan.

- *Retirement knowledge* helps you save, invest, reduce taxes and deliver a nice nest egg for your later years. It helps to clarify many of your other financial Life Planning decisions if retirement or a reduced work level is part of your Life Plan.

- *Tax knowledge* can save you money for your Life Plan year after year.

- *Insurance* can offset losses from large, sudden and unexpected occurrences that might derail your Life Plan.

- *Estate Planning and a Will* can protect and secure legacy aspects of your Life Plan so that if anything happens to you much of your Life Plan can still survive for the benefit of others.

- *Real estate* knowledge can determine the best setting for your home, as well as provide alternative forms of investment, ways to save and also to build equity for your Life Plan.

- *Knowledge of financial experts* can direct you quickly to the professional help you need for your Life Plan.

- ***Registered Life Planners*** in particular are usually Certified Financial Planners® or in the UK Chartered Financial Planners who are trained to facilitate both your Life Plan and your financial requirements.

Knowledge determines the strength of the financial architecture that supports your Life Plan, but it is your Life Plan itself that allows you to flourish. Together they form your financial Life Plan. They support each other. The financial plan brings greater confidence toward the accomplishment of the Life Plan.

It is in Knowledge that we are launched securely into the rest of our life, the life we have always wished to live, with a real road map we call the financial Life Plan.

Louis' Story

Louis' Knowledge meeting with Ben and Anita was all charts and graphs with spreadsheets, cash flows and business plans integrating and intermingling. It crackled with energy. Ben had secured and taken a job as interim manager for a retail business. Both Ben and Anita had first drafts of business plans that Louis quickly adapted to the spreadsheets he'd done on 12 month cash flow projections under various scenarios. Ben's new position paid well even on four days a week. Their cash flow looked solid; Ben had begun a new fitness regime; Anita was actively engaged with Carlo, and for the first time in their lives they became aware that the businesses they were creating, if successful and well executed, might have value in the future – sale value, retirement value.

"I clearly recall the two of you coming in; it seems just a few weeks ago," Louis said. "I've watched you move from totally lost and desperate to goal oriented, strategized and planned with a lot of vigor to execute on," Louis said.

Ben and Anita looked at each other with a very satisfied look, knowing that this was true and feeling extraordinarily good about it.

Louis' meeting with Ben and Anita was really a combination of a Knowledge meeting with all its charts and analyses, and an Execution meeting with its celebrations of a life and financial plan acted upon and achieved.

Self-Help

Knowledge is the phase of financial Life Planning where most of us are relieved to have the help of a financial professional—someone unbiased, a fiduciary, someone who clearly places the client's interests first, without conflicts of interest, someone with a breadth of financial understanding along with an authentic capacity to connect with their clients' dreams and aspirations. But for many of us, our distrust of the financial industry is too great a barrier to overcome. It's why our final chapter lays out in some detail how you can find a financial adviser you can both trust and afford!

That said, if we want to work without an adviser, what can we do as individuals that might approximate the sophistication of the software and analyses that a great financial adviser will have at their fingertips?

Typically the excitement of a Knowledge meeting is to see in print the goals, their time frames for accomplishment, the cash flow and net worth statements and projections that capture the Life Plan going forward, along with a list of actions remaining to accomplish both the financial and personal sides of the plan. In a financial Life Planner's office, the plan can be quite comprehensive, but is always clear and concise about the action steps remaining and how and when they are to be accomplished. If you are working without an adviser, you want to end up with the same kind of detailed, ready-to-implement action plan.

Your Personal Financial Life Plan

Financial Knowledge is vast, and our personal lives are of infinite variety. We could never adequately capture either of them in a chapter of this size, or indeed of any size. What we can do is provide you with a framework that will enable you each to do your own workmanlike job creating a financial plan for yourself that will bring your Life Plan to life, an approximation really of what a great financial planner would be able to deliver, but lacking much of their sophistication and detail. Here and in the final chapter, we will point you toward resources, approaches and professionals you may want to consult that would add the sophistication and detail you may desire or require.

The financial Life Plan will be based on two timelines, linked to your work in the Exploration, Vision and Obstacles phases that will identify significant events you expect or aspire to in your life. Each of these events can then be approached with a modified retirement calculator, that will shed light on how secure your Life Plan is for that event, not to mention the rest of your life. Finally, we will include a set of skills, suggestions and approaches that will enable you to strengthen the financial side of your Life Plan in innumerable ways to fit your own personal circumstances.

The Two Timelines

One of the ways to bridge the gap between the personal goals of the Life Plan and the more practical work of the financial plan is to fill out the first timeline grid we call Goals for Your Life. As you look at the grid below, feel free to change the timelines or to add rows with your own categories, or to change the categories we've used, if there's something you feel would speak more to you and your situation.

Please fill in each relevant box with your goals and your action steps that will accomplish them. You don't need to fill in every box, but make sure to include all the goals and actions steps you already recorded in Obstacles.

Goals for Your Life Plan

	One Week	One Month	Three Months	One Year	Three Years	Five Years	Ten Years	Twenty Years	Lifetime
Work									
Family									
Relationship									
Spirit									
Community									
Creativity									
Health									

For the second timeline, take those goals from the Goals for Your Life grid that imply significant financial events, both positive and negative, for your life – events that will either deliver or demand significant amounts of time or money. Some that come to mind:

- buying a home
- paying off debt
- having a child
- changing careers
- finishing school
- taking a sabbatical year
- receiving an inheritance
- working part time
- retiring
- receiving social security

Match these and kinds of significant events from your grid with the age you anticipate they will occur, using a chart like the one below. With each of these events you will then want to apply the retirement calculator that we will talk about next.

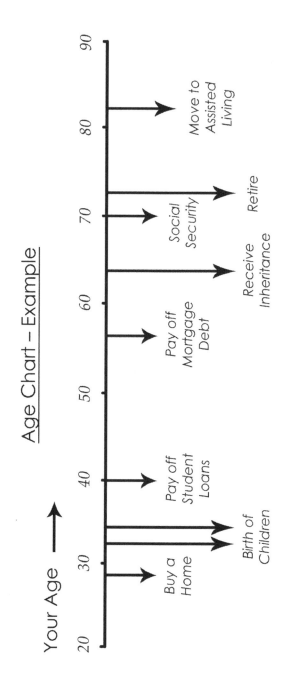

Age Chart – Example

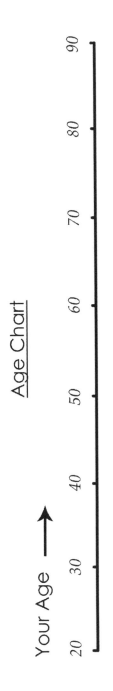

Age Chart

Your Age →

20   30   40   50   60   70   80   90

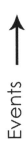

Events →

A Financial Architecture Safeguarding Retirement: The Retirement Calculator or BERT

It is challenging for most of us to keep up with and integrate all the financial knowledge necessary to create a financial plan for ourselves. In this chapter we just scratch the surface of that knowledge. But that's what Life Planning comes to and must deliver in the "K" of EVOKE®. The sustainable financial architecture for most of us is a financial plan. Its sophistication and complexity are part of the reason we recommend finding a financial planner you can trust, as we show you how to do in the final chapter.

It is true that many of the websites we will mention later in this chapter, including Quicken (http://quicken.intuit.com), have financial planning modules, but none of them are as robust (or complex) as professional financial planning software.

But if you still would prefer not to go to a financial adviser, I have a back of envelope financial planning approach to add to the links we'll give you. It is a retirement calculator that we affectionately call BERT, or the Back-of-the-Envelope Retirement Tool, and you'll find it on our website www.lifeplanningforyou.com. I've used this tool for many years when I've had quick questions for myself about the financial architecture supporting my own Life Plan. It's a shorthand approach and so it has multiple weaknesses, as it simplifies things, but in the times when I've contrasted its results with professional packages, I've been pleased. Simplicity, after all, has some virtues. And if you're not going to work with an adviser, I'd rather you have a seat of the pants version to work with than nothing at all.

The first step in the process is to construct a budget from your cash flow, or a series of budgets, as I talked about in my book, *The Seven Stages of Money Maturity* (1999). Your cash flow looks at the past, your budget at the future. As we've mentioned, a good Life Plan may require some economic sacrifice, certainly at the beginning, but frequently ends with the financial benefits of greater efficiencies and greater vigor in your economic life. As you construct your plan, you will want to be prepared in your budget for the sacrifice that may start it all as well as the potential benefits. So you might construct three budgets. The lean budget that will nonetheless deliver you your Life Plan no matter what, a "moderate" budget and a "fun to" budget.

There will be various issues to consider. If you are young, with little savings or in debt, you'll want to explore all the possible ways to get out of debt, increase your savings and begin to invest in ways that are likely to deliver a much stronger return than a simple savings account. We will start you on that path.

The deeper questions you will be concerned with involve how to live your Life Plan, accomplish your work/life balance, and deliver your passion for your entrepreneurial, creative and value-driven endeavors into the world. From an economic standpoint these questions will come down to the use and the rewards of your time and your money.

From my experience with thousands of people whose Life Plans I have touched, I see economic rewards that are significant, even if people take time away from their normal occupation to live their Life Plan. This is because they increase significantly their energy, vitality, optimism, clarity, their focus and happiness, and all of these qualities lead to much greater efficiencies at work. Your "moderate" and "fun to" budgets should be based on these possibilities.

Once you've identified your budgets, you'll want to look at the income side of things. The simplest approach is simply to consider what income you are making now. Contrasting your current income with the budgets, are you saving, or are you spending more than you're making? If you are still in the asset accumulation phase of your life, you will likely want to be saving and adding to your investments. You will also want to contrast your budgets to what BERT suggests you can afford to spend based upon your assets and your sources of income.

But before we get to BERT we need to consider what your investable assets can safely produce for you in terms of an annual withdrawal rate from your savings.

Investment Retirement Risk: Banish fear of 1929

Academic studies have argued for years that a balanced and diversified portfolio of 50-75% equities (stocks) 25-50% bonds can get you through the worst of economic times, even the great crash of 1929 and the depression that followed, with a 4% inflation adjusted withdrawal rate from your portfolio. The guru of this argument for many years has been William F. Bengen who argues for a 4.5% withdrawal rate. The most prolific challenger to Bengen, Wade Pfau, has added much detail and nuance to the theory, but cautions that with current stock market valuations the rate may be less than 3%. Michael Kitces and Jonathan Guyton have each made significant contributions to the discussion. All three, in fact, have suggested ways to increase these withdrawal rates. One of the most intriguing suggestions, by Pfau, involves the use of single premium immediate annuities instead of bonds. Jonathan Guyton has argued that you could get a safe withdrawal rate between 5 and 6% if you are willing to limit your withdrawals in market crises or in high inflation.

I've heard many a client respond to all this with, "Wait a minute! In 1929 my grandfather saw a stock market crash that lasted for three years and reduced stock market value by 89%. I'd be wiped out if I took out 4% per year and that were to happen again." What my clients forget is the value of diversification. If 40% of your assets were in treasuries, while the stock market was falling, your bonds were increasing in value, keeping enough of your net worth preserved for it to all take off again in 1932 when the market began its dramatic recovery.

Of course we also hear arguments when bond or money market yields are above 4% that all one's assets should be put in those "safe" investments. What the consumer doesn't realize is the added risk and the limited value of those kinds of investments coming from how they closely track inflation. If they beat inflation, it's because of additional risk that's being taken. Bonds don't generally beat inflation by much more than a percentage point, so 1% is closer to your safe withdrawal rate than 4% on a bond or money market portfolio. Moreover with the longest term bonds, those often offering the highest rates of interest, if the inflation rate doubles, the value of your portfolio of bonds will fall by nearly half.

Nowadays we have much greater opportunities for diversification than we had in the old days. We have opportunities to invest in equities that have traditionally delivered much higher than average rates of return, equities in international and emerging markets, in very small companies, in exotic categories specialists study like international small cap value. In our bond portfolios we can invest in inflation protected securities, inflation being one of the riskiest conditions for a portfolio, and in widely diversified and sophisticated annuities. Each of these can increase the rate of return for a diversified portfolio or lower the risk – often both. Most of the long-term studies have not included the benefits of these added measures of diversification on a "safe" withdrawal rate from our balanced portfolios, because our statistics don't go back to 1926 on these categories of assets as they do for blue chip stocks and bonds. Given this added diversification, my hunch is, with good advice, we will likely see the 4% standard hold for most of our portfolios. My personal advice to those living off their savings, is to take 4%, consider the use of single premium immediate annuities and have a "worst case" plan, to reduce the percentage you take during challenging economic times or as you age. This approach neatly combines the diverse approaches mentioned above. 1929 was horrible, possibly the worst market catastrophe since the great plague and the fire of London combined in the 17th century. So you have a lot of reassurance, if you know you could beat the 1929 conditions. But something worse could always come in the form of economic, health or environmental catastrophes or war, although it's hard to imagine something worse than the Great Depression sandwiched between two world wars.

BERT

Two valuable questions arise as you experiment with BERT, my Back of the Envelope Retirement Tool. What could I spend if I were to retire right now? And what could I spend when I come to my time for retirement once Social Security is available? So here's the formula, much as Lee Eisenberg reported my correspondence with him in *The Number: A Completely Different Way to Think About the Rest of Your Life* (Copyright © 2006, Free Press, A Division of Simon and Schuster).

A. Total up your invested assets (assuming they're well diversified, i.e., a 60/40 share-to-bond ratio): _____

B. Multiply A by .04, which tells you how much annual investment income you might reasonably withdraw each year (this is based on the 4% solution discussed above): _____

C. Add in the annualised value of any home equity you have (to do this, divide your total equity by the number of years you expect to live. For example, if your age is sixty, and you have $400,000 in home equity, and expect to live to be one hundred, the annual value of your real estate would be $10,000): _____

D. Add any income you expect from inheritances (again, total inheritance divided by the number of years you expect to live): _____

E. Add the amount of social security you assume you're entitled to per year (for help, visit www.ssa.gov): _____

F. Add any expected annual pension or annuity benefits: _____

G. Add any remaining income you expect per year, including from your job or part-time work, rentals and all other sources: _____

H. Total B to G, and you arrive at how much you can spend each year to get through the rest of your life: _____

If you find that your assets and income are insufficient, then you will want to continue to accumulate assets, as described later in this chapter, or cut back expenses. Whether you are already retired or not, you will want to factor in changing life circumstances into your budgets and into these equations: paying off your mortgage, kids leaving home, education bills settled, commuting requirements eliminated, new car or roof to be purchased, the date social security begins for you. This may involve running separate BERTs for different time periods in your life.

Throughout my life, I always figured that if I could at least find a way to live safely on my lean budget (regardless of my moderate or fun budgets), from then on my primary focus should be on living my Life Plan. Accumulating assets might be a part of that plan, but it was unlikely to occupy the sacred spot of Question Three.

A great adviser would do the same for you, finding the most sensible and economic way for you to flourish into your Life Plan. Without sacrificing basic economic sense, it is your Life Plan that you must live, and all these figures are ultimately meant to support it. It is living our Life Plans that makes our lives worth living. Our finances should be designed to support them, not to take from them.

Alternative Uses for BERT

One of the things I love about BERT is its flexibility. Plugging in the figures (even if I can't yet collect Social Security) I can determine how much money I can retire on right now. If I'm close to retirement age and I don't have quite enough to retire on, but Social Security will take me well over my retirement needs in just a few years, I might be able to retire now anyway, overspending a bit on my assets for now, but then saving some annually to put into my investment portfolio each year once I start receiving Social Security. The formula can also be used to give me great insight whether I should begin to collect Social Security at 62, 66 or 70, although much of that decision will be based on my health and expected longevity. You might look for calculators on the web such as www.ssa.gov/OACT/quickcalc/ to aid in your personal Social Security timeline decisions.

When I was a young man I used the retirement calculator to strategize how I might move to a foreign country living on the cheap while I wrote the books I most wanted to write. At that time it was Costa Rica that looked most appealing, although now it might be Nicaragua or Ecuador or a country in South East Asia. I'd saved a small amount and figured at a minimum I could sell my Income Tax practice for one times my gross income. The formula told me how much I had to increase my tax practice in order to retire to a simple life of writing in Latin America. Nowadays for someone with computer skills, working remotely on a part time basis could set up a similar 'retirement' even more quickly. Of course BERT can also be used with one's budget to determine how one might switch from a full to a part-time job here in the states as well, or to explore if one can afford to take an unpaid sabbatical to tour the world, to change careers, buy a home or have another child.

One of the areas of flexibility in the retirement calculator (BERT) that can be creatively used is real estate. I wrestled with real estate for the longest time as I worked with the early versions of BERT, figuring and refiguring ways real estate equity might be added to the income on which one might retire. So many financial advisers choose to ignore equity in a client's home for retirement purposes, given the common desire to live out one's golden years in one's own home. The advent of reverse mortgages that allow one to continue to live at home while collecting money from the bank for the home's equity, opened my thinking, even with all their financial limitations. Also I wanted to consider the reality that many end up living their final years in assisted living or in a much smaller home than they used in the middle of their life. Many also think of their home equity as a nest egg, completely outside of any retirement formula, flexible and available in unforeseen circumstances, for fun or for emergency.

How, as well, could I account for the varying rates at which equity increases in real estate? For instance if the real estate is highly leveraged, your equity is likely to increase at a much higher rate than inflation, whereas if you own your home outright, the equity is likely to grow only slightly better than inflation. And of course there are the very rare periods historically, like the one we've just gone through, where real estate plummets in value. How could I capture all of these possibilities in BERT? Well, of course, I couldn't. But you can, if you know more about your likely use of your property. For instance, would you like to consider it as a nest egg, and ignore it in the formula entirely? Or ignore half the equity? You can do either. Or would you like to be conservative and make sure you can live in your property for your entire life? You can do that by increasing your life expectancy in the formula to a ripe old age far longer than you think is remotely realistic. Or, perhaps you are highly leveraged, and see the equity in your home growing even faster than the equity in your investments. You might then ignore the real estate line of the calculator, and instead put the equity amount into your total sum of investable assets subject to the 4% solution.

The real estate formula as I've set it up assumes a quite conservative approach. It assumes that your equity right now will not grow, but will remain constant in real inflation-adjusted dollars, and it divides your use of that equity over the expected remaining years of your life. Feel free to adjust the formula as you like, more conservative or more aggressive, as you feel most comfortable, and as fits the requirements of your Life Plan.

The Four Ways to Accumulate Assets

The first step toward the financial freedom of our Life Plan, for many of us, involves accumulating assets or getting out of debt. Indeed what BERT often reveals is that our ideal level of expenses is more than our income and assets can afford. I think of accumulating assets as "building your freedom." Certainly it builds financial freedom. And as you build this layer of freedom you have much greater flexibility in your choice of Life Plans, as well as a much stronger financial foundation for your Life Plan. As a tax accountant and later as a financial planner and investment manager, I observed four major ways that clients accumulated assets. Each of them increased their ability to save and invest.

For most of us, our assets will grow most through investing in the stock market, increasing our equity in our home, or building our own business. None of these are without risk. Here are four broad approaches that can help us to leverage our asset accumulation and gain flexibility in our Life Plan.

1. *Simplify your life and save money (and invest!)*

This is one of the most basic yet brilliant of ideas: cut out clutter, eliminate time-wasting tasks, think of every possible way that you can save time and money to bring more flexibility to your Life Plan. This can work in unison with the other ideas we share here, or all by itself it can be the fundamental economic principal behind your Life Plan. For most people I know this has been the backbone of their movement toward economic freedom. Mary Rowland has neighbors in New York's Hudson Valley, Marc Eisenson and Nancy Castleman, who live this idea and have written a book about it, *Invest in Yourself: The Six Secrets to a Rich Life* (1998). Another popular book is Vicki Robin's *Your Money or Your Life: Transforming Your Relationship with Money and Achieving Financial Independence* (1999).

Most of us long for a simpler life, but few execute it. Here's your chance. Simplifying can give you more money to invest or to get out of debt. Or it can mean more time to pursue your life's passion, your Life Plan, your dream of freedom.

Here is a link to a *Simple Living Manifesto,* which contains links to dozens of other articles and books on simplifying your life:

- http://zenhabits.net/simple-living-manifesto-72-ideas-to-simplify-your-life/

As well as another website on *Project Simplify*:

- http://projectsimplify.com/articles/creating-a-simplicity-statement/

Later in this chapter, and in the final chapter, I will go over the ways that saving can turn to investing, and that investing can help to accumulate assets rapidly. The most important asset investing accumulates of course, is your Life Plan.

2. *Leverage your home*

I'd like to say a word or two more about real estate and the banking crises. Real estate is historically one of the more stable of the risky investments, far more stable than stocks. Part of that is because a seller, rather than responding to current market pressures can choose to wait sometimes weeks or months for the right price. So one of the measures that is analyzed in real estate is how quickly properties are selling or how long they are sitting on the market. As a consequence, the real estate market tends not to fall as far or as fast as one might expect given market or economic conditions. That said, this is not the world's experience of real estate over the last few years, where at first real estate soared and then it collapsed. This unusual boom and bust in real estate is a, literally, once in a life time phenomenon, in this case brought on by speculative fervor from loose credit as we approached a banking crisis and credit collapse.

Consumer psychology in fluctuating markets, whether stocks or real estate, is rather odd. When a market has been going up strongly for quite a while, consumers (often supported by the media) find a way to believe that it will go up forever. Everyone seems to jump into the market just as it's about to turn down. Thus when the market crashes it can be quite devastating. Before it crashes, many people go into debt and pour their life savings into the frenzied market. This is one of the reasons we recommend finding an adviser you can trust, someone who will keep you diversified, rather than over-extended, or gambling on a single asset class.

Of course the reverse is true as well. When markets have been going down for quite some time, you hear people swearing off stocks or real estate forever. When everyone agrees how risky things are and you have a selling frenzy, you've usually reached a market bottom, just the time to buy not sell.

Long before the current market crisis and long before Standard & Poor's began to put together a real estate index called the Case-Shiller index that details price fluctuations in real estate, I would hand out a chart of 20th Century land price fluctuations to my Life Planning clients.

I used it to show my over-eager clients how real estate could turn against them. It was astonishing to see the period from 1919 to 1932 when land values fell consistently and then dramatically.

"But that's ancient history," my clients would say or "that's land, not real estate" or "things have changed, real estate always goes up." And indeed for most of the 75 years after 1932, it looked as if they were right.

Prices tend to collapse in banking crises, or just before, when credit is squeezed. "Debt deflation" defines a time when the total amount of debt in a society is reduced. Banking crises don't come along very often but when they do they're devastating, worse than any recession. And come along they do. In fact they're inevitable as long as politicians have access to the money supply and can increase it to help themselves get elected. With a great deal of consistency, every four years after a banking crisis the total level of debt (government plus corporate plus consumer) gets a bit worse until at some point, decades after the last crisis (the Great Depression in this case), there is a frenzy of leverage, increasing asset values (stocks or real estate, or electric companies or railroads or tulips; it can be almost anything) followed by a devastating collapse, where everyone who participated in the frenzy loses.

For the past few years, consumers have been as overly skeptical about real estate as they were unrealistically optimistic about it before the crisis began. But when the selling frenzy is complete (and you still hear arguments both ways about where in the cycle we are now), real estate will return to do what it does, and what it did for most of the last century. Real estate is a commodity that serves a growing population that has only a limited amount of land. So it tends to match inflation plus a bit. And it's a good investment.

Traditionally, one of the quickest ways to accumulate money has been to invest in real estate. For most Americans this has meant leveraging your investment in your home with a good sized mortgage. When you purchase a home, you might buy it by putting 20 percent down and borrowing the other 80 percent. Suppose you buy a $250,000 home with a down payment of $50,000. You are "investing" that $50,000 in a home with the possibility of doubling your investment – or perhaps more than doubling. Say you live in the home for several years, then sell it for $300,000. After you pay off the mortgage, your $50,000 has doubled to $100,000. This "leverage your home" strategy would not have worked over the first decade of the twenty-first century but that is the only period since 1932 when it wouldn't have worked, because housing prices headed down for the first time in 70 years in 2003 and 2004.

If you enjoy making home improvements, you can increase the speed of your leverage, by doing these fix-up tasks that add additional value to your balance sheet.

I have a good friend who loves to landscape and fix up properties slowly, as he lives in them. For 20 years, every three to four years, he would turn around and sell the home he lived in, pocketing four to five times the down payment he'd made on the property each time.

Here are some useful links:

- http://www.ehow.com/how_2107860_use-home-equity-as-leverage.html

- http://homeguides.sfgate.com/leverage-real-estate-equity-9212.html

- http://voices.yahoo.com/what-leverage-entrepreneur-leverage-5281595.html

- http://www.bankrate.com/calculators/mortgages/rent-or-buy-home.aspx?ec_id=m1026159

The tax law regarding the treatment of gains in the sale of a home provides a real boost to this strategy. In the US, when you sell your home, you may exclude $250,000 of the gain ($500,000 for a married couple filing jointly) from taxes. To qualify for this tax treatment, you must have used the home as your primary residence in at least two of the past five years and you cannot use the exclusion if you have used it on another home in the past two years.

- http://homebuying.about.com/od/taxes/qt/081808_TaxBreak.htm

3. *Mine all the benefits of being self-employed*

It's true that when you work for yourself, you don't get perks like paid health benefits, vacation, holidays and retirement plans. But the advantages to being self-employed are great. You should grasp all that you can.

Among the obvious benefits are the ability to work from home and set your own hours; you are rewarded with consistent family time, the absence of the expense and time of commuting, fewer clothing needs, reduced wear-and-tear on your car and the freedom to define how and when you will pursue the essence of your Life Plan. You can arrange your time so that you devote your best time to your most important tasks. You're also likely to work more efficiently.

In addition to the greater freedom and reduced expenses that can come with self-employment, there are other financial and tax benefits. You can and should set up your own retirement account and contribute tax-deferred money every year. You may find health insurance through an association that serves your profession or industry. All of the health insurance premiums you pay are tax deductible. If you qualify, you can deduct the cost of using your home as an office. Office furniture is deductible as well.

Think of all the other expenses related to self-employment, which might include books and magazines for your business, taking a client out for dinner, going to conventions and conferences and meetings that relate to bettering your business. It also includes courses you take to improve skills for your business including social media, software engineering, Photoshop/writing, and whatever else you need for your profession. As you go through the year, keep track of all these expenses, including taxis and public transportation. Check out the rules on deducting mileage for your own car as well. Your business expenses can be deducted from your business income. See:

- http://www.bankrate.com/finance/money-guides/a-dozen-deductions-for-your-small-business-1.aspx

- http://www.investopedia.com/articles/tax/09/self-employed-tax-deductions.asp#axzz1wBfnRo58

- http://www.taxpreparerplus.com/self_employed.html

Perhaps the greatest economic benefit for many of you who are self-employed will come if you are able to structure your business in such a way that you can sell it. Many professional businesses can be sold for at least one times your annual gross income, but it can take careful planning to set this up, and the range of values for a business can be quite large – from nothing to several times gross. If you are self-employed, this is well worth a consultation with both an accountant and a financial adviser.

4. *Mine all the benefits of being an employee*

When Mary Rowland's daughter got her first job out of college as a graphic designer she sent her new benefits package to Mary. Mary was floored. Her plan included health insurance but also full dental insurance, gym membership, seminars on financial, emotional and physical wellness and onsite yoga year round as well as free massage, nutrition and financial management consulting. The company paid a portion of college tuition and employees could get equity in the company, a bonus, and company contributions to the 401(k) plan. New employees got 3.2 weeks of vacation the first year. All employees shared in tickets to sports events, music and theater and discounts were offered on many things, including Zip-Car.

Although not all companies are this generous and many have cut back on benefits in the past decade, ask for a copy of the employee benefits handbook and be sure to take advantage of all that are offered. Most companies offer an "open enrollment" program once a year during which you can sign up for benefits. Don't miss it. During that period, sign up for deductions to your company 401(k) plan as well. If your company matches any part of your contribution, make it! If you don't, you're leaving money on the table.

Benefits can include disability insurance, healthcare, overtime and vacation time, maternity leave, educational benefits, and holidays and weekends off. In defining and choosing to live your Life Plan you will want to weigh these benefits versus the benefits you receive when you are self-employed. I've seen employees with good salaries and great benefits accelerate their movement toward their Life Plan by living modestly, saving a high percentage of their salaries and then when they're ready, moving more aggressively into their Life Plan with all the added flexibility additional savings can bring.

- http://www.bankrate.com/finance/personal-finance/how-to-make-the-most-of-employee-benefits-1.aspx

- http://www.money-zine.com/Career-Development/Finding-a-Job/Top-Employee-Benefits/

- http://www.wisegeek.com/what-are-employee-benefits.htm

Additional Considerations

As you accumulate assets and build strength in your BERT, it makes sense to consider the five categories of finance that form the basis of a Certified Financial Planner® designation: Insurance/risk, taxes, investing, retirement and estate planning. Each will be helpful in their own way toward your Life Plan by increasing your assets, by protecting them from disaster or by securing your legacy.

Do not become discouraged if as you do your budget or begin to save, when you add up what you own and what you owe, you see that there's not much owning and lots of owing. As you become determined to live your Life Plan, often the first financial step is to bring down debt. Although the debt may now be a burden, for most of us at one point debt enabled us to grow, to go to school, to live where we want, to start a business, to gain experiences that have made us a richer person.

I think it's important to see your "human capital" as part of your investments and assets. Human capital increases when you add education, skills, experience in management or computer skills and social media expertise among the many things you do to become a more valuable person or employee or when you start your own business.

As we pay off debt we are building terrific financial muscle. They are the same muscles that enable us to build up savings, and the same we need in order to live within a budget. Our increased personal strength secures our Life Plan step by step, every time we exercise those muscles.

One major error that people without a financial plan make is that they believe they are choosing between only two things: Buying a motorcycle or upgrading the stereo system. The third option is: Buy nothing today and put that money toward a secure Life Plan and toward your longer-term goals. In fact whenever you're tempted to spend a significant amount on a new venture, consider first: Will this new expenditure take me further from my Life Plan or bring me directly to it. The whole point of saving and accumulating assets is to deliver you into your Life Plan.

Now let's look at the five areas of financial knowledge required for a Certified Financial Planner® designation and see how you might benefit from these yourself.

Five Areas of Financial Planning

1. Insurance and risk management

The biggest risk that we all face is that we won't get to live the life we feel meant to live. Life Planning is the process that addresses that risk directly. Insurance is meant to cover the next biggest risks, the devastating and sudden financial losses that can bring our Life Plan to ruin in moments. The general rule on insurance is not to waste money insuring small things, cover those with your own savings and prudence. But make sure you've secured your Life Plan against the truly major disasters.

Everyone understands how life insurance helps the dependents manage the risk that the policyholder will die by providing a tax-free insurance benefit to the survivors. If part of your Life Plan is to support those who depend on your income, you need life insurance. To get started, buy term insurance. This is a simple policy that guarantees to pay your beneficiary the face value if you die within the term. You can buy 1-year, 10-year, 20-year term, as well as other term periods. The younger you are, the cheaper it is. If your children are young, you might consider 20-year term.

How much insurance do you need? A financial adviser would probably suggest 20 times your dependents' annual income needs. You can find insurance worksheets on many websites such as:

- http://finance.yahoo.com/news/purchase-life-insurance-160621858. html

- http://finance.yahoo.com/calculator/insurance/ins01/

- http://www.kiplinger.com/magazine/archives/how-much-life-insurance-do-you-need.html

You will also need homeowner's insurance, auto insurance, perhaps an umbrella liability policy that pays excess liability beyond homeowner's and auto. But make sure you are insuring against the major disasters that, for instance, liability protection gives you, rather than the smaller things like "loss of use" of your car while it's in the shop. Often, as our savings grow, we increase our deductibles in our insurance policies, figuring we can cover that much of the loss ourselves, and keeping the insurance costs low to just cover major losses.

You might also look at a long-term care policy although these policies have become controversial so be sure to do your research. For more information, check here:

http://moneywatch.bnet.com/retirement-planning/blog/ money-life/should-you-buy-long-term-care-insurance/1258/

When you are young, the biggest economic risk you face is loss of your income or your ability to earn income. Financial planners say the most often overlooked area of planning is disability insurance. "It's probably the most important insurance you can buy," says Harold Evensky, a financial planner in Miami, Florida. "The biggest risk to people in their working years is that they're going to be disabled."

Many employees assume that they have coverage at work and that they don't need to buy their own policy. That's wrong. For one thing, few people spend a career at the same company. You must plan to take care of yourself. Relying on your employer's policy could leave you without coverage if you lose your job, your employer changes policies or the insurer drops your employer. Most employer policies cover only a short-term disability. Your risk is that you will not be able to work for months – or even years.

Further, if you buy your own policy the benefits are tax-free. If your employer pays the premium, your benefits are taxable. In order to buy a policy, you must have good health and an income. If you wait until you need it, you may not qualify. If you plan to leave your employer at some point, you should make certain to get a disability policy before you leave.

For more information on disability policies and long-term care policies go to:

- http://www.investorguide.com/igu-article-336-disability-insurance-understanding-disability-and-long-term-care-insurance-policies.html

2. *Save and Invest*

First, set up a cash flow statement. Whether you need to save or you want to monitor your income and expenses a cash flow comes in handy. For a saver, it's nearly essential. The secret to improving cash flow, of course, is simple: spend less than you earn. Whether you have a financial adviser or not, only you can decide to do that. With the fire of the Torch of your Life Plan, you are more likely to accomplish this. An excellent website to help you organize and categorize your expenses is www.mint.com.

First, list your sources of income and how much you get from each as well as your total income. Then set up a list of your annual expenses such as housing and property taxes, utilities, insurance, car loan or lease payments, education costs and other fixed expenses.

Then list discretionary or variable expenses such as food and dining out, transportation and car maintenance, entertainment and recreation, medical expenses, home maintenance, furnishings and supplies, clothing, travel and vacation, gifts and charity and other variable expenses. Finally, you must pay income tax so list that under expenses. When you subtract your expenses from your income, you will see how much you have left, which is available for savings toward your goals. Of course, you can also examine your discretionary spending to see where you could cut back to reach goals more quickly.

If you can't figure out where your money goes from your cash flow statement, sit down with three months worth of credit card bills, your check register and your withdrawal receipts from the ATM. Sort them into categories. If you can't remember what you bought with the cash withdrawals from the ATM, begin writing your purchases on each receipt. Groceries? Movies? Paintball? Museums? BlackRock Casino? After you've collected these annotated receipts for a month, go back and look over them to see where your money is going. If you're not happy with it, you can change it!

One of our advisers in the UK, Jeremy Deedes, enthusiastically recommends the personal finance software Moneydance.com (www. moneydance.com). He calls it the "high tech/high touch" approach to monitoring cash flow. It uses simplified accounting terms to keep track of monthly expenses, account balances, savings and investments, and payment due dates. He also endorses Voyant software to estimate lifetime cash flow and "what if" scenarios, describing it as a product where "life meets the money." And there are others.

• www.planwithvoyant.com/content/consumer/default/index.html

Save money. As much as you can. Even though interest rates have been hovering around zero in the years since the 2008 financial crash, putting money in savings still makes sense. After paying off debt, putting money in a savings account should be your next step. If you regularly accumulate money in a savings account, you'll soon have enough to invest.

Pay yourself first. The best way to build savings is to arrange for a certain amount of money to be withheld from each paycheck and deposited into a savings or retirement account such as a 401(k) plan at work. If that's not available, put it in an IRA or a savings account at your bank.

If you work for a company that has a credit union, check out the rates there. Credit unions generally pay a bit higher interest than a bank.

It's also nearly painless to have money withheld from your paycheck and deposited in savings. Members of credit unions usually get better rates on loans as well.

* http://www.getrichslowly.org/blog/2009/10/19/pay-yourself-first/

* http://www.investopedia.com/terms/p/payyourselffirst. asp#axzz1bjAuSFCG

Pay off debt. Now that you know where your money is going, you can make some decisions about whether you are using your money to reach your most important goals.

If you owe money on credit cards or consumer loans, your top priority will likely be to pay that off. There is no place you can earn as high a guaranteed return as by paying off debt. If your credit card carries a 10% interest rate, by paying it down you earn 10% on that money. Few cards have such low rates today. Many are 20 percent plus, which makes paying off debt a no-brainer.

If you owe money on several credit cards, list the amount and the interest rate on each. If you can conveniently transfer balances to your lowest rate card, do it! Consolidate. If not, concentrate on the one with the highest interest rate. Pay the minimums on the others and put everything else you can afford to pay on the highest rate card. That way you will earn the best return on your money. When that card is paid off, concentrate on the second highest rate card and so on until you have paid off your debt. If you are serious about living your Life Plan, you will be eager to get rid of these obstacles in your path.

My favorite credit/debt expert is Gerri Detweiler, who has been writing about credit for 25 years. You can find her at credit.com as well as many other websites. She's also written several books about credit.

* http://www.credit.com/blog/2011/10/3-steps-to-clear-your-credit-card-debt/

Invest wisely. This is most important. A good investment strategy implemented for decades has been the most successful approach to accumulating assets outside of the equity in your home.

Investing can be done in your pensions and retirement programs or simply by saving and investing directly. As you work with BERT over the different time periods of your life, you may want to consider having assets available for the 4% solution both during retirement and before. We've shared with you some of the basics about the stock, bond and money markets (short-term bond markets) and their relative risks. Although equities provide by far the highest long-term rate of return, you will want to diversify in order to lower the risk of stock market volatility. Equity represents ownership, like that you have in your house or stocks. Volatility (another term for risk) is greater for stocks, but the long-term return on stocks far exceeds the inflation-adjusted return on bonds, CDs, real estate or money market accounts. When you compound this higher average rate of return over a lifetime, the assets accumulate much faster than nearly all other forms of investment. At the same time, diversification will lessen the risk and reduce the overall volatility of your investments.

One of the easiest and cheapest ways to invest in stocks is to buy index funds or exchange-traded funds that represent some market index or some standardized segment of the stock or bond market. Time was when the only indexes available were those based on one sector of the market. Today you can buy an index to invest in almost anything. We will discuss passive (the index fund approach) and active investing in our final chapter. In addition, see our Books to Further Your Investment Knowledge page at the end of the book for a bibliography focused on investing.

Some of you may be wondering why diversify? Wouldn't you make more money by just being in stocks when they are going up and out of them in something safe when they are going down? Well of course. The problem is, no one has been able to figure out how to do that consistently, and most of the smartest people in investing understand that you can't. If someone could figure out how, soon everyone would be following them. And if everyone's buying at the same time, who's selling? And what happens then to the price?

Instead, wise investors have learned that diversification is your friend, and can bring you many of the benefits of equity investing, without nearly as much of the threat of market collapse. Consider this chart showing which category of equity or bond did best in each of the last 20 years. You will see the categories bouncing around so much that I hope you realize how impossible it is to predict, and how valuable diversification is as an alternative. One of the advantages of an adviser is that they will have access to and be up to date on all the latest studies on how to diversify for best rate of return, safest portfolio structure and safest withdrawal rates in retirement.

We tend to think that keeping our assets in a simple savings account is safest, and that is likely to be true, if we are saving for vacation or a bicycle we want to buy in the next year or so. But if we're saving for our Life Plan, or for retirement, or require distributions in retirement, broad diversification including the stock market will be a much safer alternative, giving us protection against taxes and inflation that a simple savings account might not, and giving us the opportunity to grow our portfolio as well.

I mentioned earlier that the 4% solution generally requires 50-75% in equities. So which should it be, 50 or 75? Or somewhere in between? If I'm a risk taker I'd put 75% of my investible assets in equities, 25% in bonds. If I'm risk-averse I'd go 50/50. Most of us should be somewhere in between. In addition I'd be looking to have about a third of my total net worth in property or my home – more if I'm handy with property, or it's part of my business. Often advisers these days are putting a third or more of the equity portion of their portfolio in international funds. Studying the chart, you can see why.

The Callan Periodic Table of Investment Returns

Annual Returns for Key Indices Ranked in Order of Performance (1994–2013)

1994	1995	1996	1997	1998	1999	2000	2001	2002	2003	2004	2005	2006	2007	2008	2009	2010	2011	2012	2013
MSCI EAFE 7.78%	S&P 500 Growth 38.13%	S&P 500 Growth 23.97%	S&P 500 Growth 36.52%	S&P 500 Growth 42.16%	MSCI Emerging Markets 66.42%	Russell 2000 Value 22.83%	Russell 2000 Value 14.02%	Barclays Agg 10.26%	MSCI Emerging Markets 55.26%	MSCI Emerging Markets 25.95%	MSCI Emerging Markets 34.54%	MSCI Emerging Markets 32.59%	MSCI Emerging Markets 39.78%	Barclays Agg 5.24%	MSCI Emerging Markets 79.02%	Russell 2000 Growth 29.09%	Barclays Agg 7.84%	MSCI Emerging Markets 18.63%	Russell 2000 Growth 43.30%
S&P 500 Growth 3.13%	S&P 500 37.58%	S&P 500 22.96%	S&P 500 33.36%	S&P 500 28.58%	Russell 2000 Growth 43.09%	Barclays Agg 11.63%	Barclays Agg 8.43%	Barclays Corp High Yield -1.41%	Russell 2000 Growth 48.54%	Russell 2000 Value 22.25%	MSCI EAFE 13.54%	MSCI EAFE 26.34%	MSCI EAFE 11.17%	Barclays Corp High Yield -26.16%	Barclays Corp High Yield 58.21%	Russell 2000 26.85%	Barclays Corp High Yield 4.98%	Russell 2000 Value 18.05%	Russell 2000 38.82%
S&P 500 1.32%	S&P 500 Value 36.99%	S&P 500 Value 22.00%	Russell 2000 Value 31.78%	MSCI EAFE 20.00%	S&P 500 Growth 28.24%	S&P 500 Value 6.08%	Barclays Corp High Yield 5.28%	MSCI Emerging Markets -6.00%	Russell 2000 47.25%	MSCI EAFE 20.25%	S&P 500 Value 5.82%	Russell 2000 Value 23.48%	S&P 500 Growth 9.13%	Russell 2000 Value -28.92%	Russell 2000 Growth 34.47%	Russell 2000 Value 24.50%	S&P 500 Growth 4.65%	S&P 500 Value 17.68%	Russell 2000 Value 34.52%
S&P 500 Value -0.64%	Russell 2000 Growth 31.04%	Russell 2000 21.37%	S&P 500 Value 29.98%	S&P 500 Value 14.69%	MSCI EAFE 26.96%	Russell 2000 -3.02%	Russell 2000 2.49%	Russell 2000 Value -11.43%	Russell 2000 Value 46.03%	Russell 2000 18.33%	S&P 500 4.91%	S&P 500 Value 20.81%	Russell 2000 Growth 7.05%	Russell 2000 -33.79%	MSCI EAFE 31.78%	MSCI Emerging Markets 19.20%	S&P 500 2.11%	MSCI EAFE 17.32%	S&P 500 Growth 32.75%
Barclays Corp High Yield -1.03%	Russell 2000 28.45%	Russell 2000 16.49%	Russell 2000 22.36%	Barclays Agg 8.70%	Russell 2000 21.26%	Barclays Corp High Yield -5.86%	MSCI Emerging Markets -2.37%	MSCI EAFE -15.94%	MSCI EAFE 38.59%	S&P 500 Value 15.71%	Russell 2000 Value 4.71%	Russell 2000 18.37%	Barclays Agg 6.97%	S&P 500 Growth -34.92%	S&P 500 Growth 31.57%	Barclays Corp High Yield 15.12%	S&P 500 Value -0.48%	Russell 2000 16.35%	S&P 500 32.39%
Russell 2000 Value -1.54%	Russell 2000 Value 25.75%	Barclays Corp High Yield 11.35%	Russell 2000 Growth 12.95%	Barclays Corp High Yield 1.87%	S&P 500 21.04%	S&P 500 -9.11%	Russell 2000 Growth -9.23%	Russell 2000 -20.48%	S&P 500 Value 31.79%	Russell 2000 Growth 14.31%	Russell 2000 4.55%	S&P 500 15.79%	S&P 500 5.49%	S&P 500 -37.00%	Russell 2000 27.17%	S&P 500 Value 15.10%	Russell 2000 Growth -2.91%	S&P 500 16.00%	S&P 500 Value 31.99%

	1	2	3	4	5	6	7	8	9	10	11	12	13	14	15	16	17	18	19
Rank 1	Russell 2000 −1.82%	Barclays Corp High Yield 19.18%	Russell 2000 Growth 11.26%	Barclays Corp High Yield 12.76%	S&P 500 Value 12.73%	MSCI EAFE −14.17%	S&P 500 Value −11.71%	S&P 500 Value −20.85%	Barclays Corp High Yield 28.97%	Barclays Corp High Yield 11.13%	Russell 2000 Growth 4.15%	Russell 2000 Growth 13.35%	S&P 500 Value 1.99%	Russell 2000 Growth −38.54%	S&P 500 26.47%	S&P 500 15.06%	Russell 2000 −4.18%	Barclays Corp High Yield 15.81%	MSCI EAFE 22.76%
Rank 2	Russell 2000 Growth −2.43%	Barclays Agg 18.46%	MSCI EAFE 6.05%	Barclays Agg 9.64%	Barclays Corp High Yield 2.39%	S&P 500 Growth −22.08%	S&P 500 −11.89%	S&P 500 Growth −22.10%	S&P 500 28.68%	S&P 500 10.88%	S&P 500 Growth 4.00%	Barclays Corp High Yield 11.85%	Russell 2000 1.87%	S&P 500 Value −39.22%	S&P 500 Growth 21.17%	S&P 500 Growth 15.05%	Russell 2000 Value −5.50%	S&P 500 Growth 14.61%	Barclays Corp High Yield 7.44%
Rank 3	Barclays Agg −2.92%	MSCI EAFE 11.21%	MSCI Emerging Markets 6.03%	MSCI EAFE 1.78%	Barclays Agg −0.82%	Russell 2000 Growth −22.43%	S&P 500 Growth −12.73%	S&P 500 −23.59%	S&P 500 Growth 25.66%	S&P 500 Growth 6.13%	Russell 2000 2.74%	S&P 500 Growth 11.01%	Russell 2000 −1.57%	MSCI EAFE −43.38%	Russell 2000 Value 20.58%	MSCI EAFE 7.75%	MSCI EAFE −12.14%	Russell 2000 Growth 14.59%	MSCI −2.02%
Rank 4	MSCI Emerging Markets −7.12%	MSCI Emerging Markets −5.21%	Barclays Agg 3.04%	MSCI Emerging Markets −11.59%	Russell 2000 Value −1.49%	MSCI Emerging Markets −30.61%	MSCI EAFE −21.44%	Russell 2000 Growth −30.26%	Barclays Agg 4.10%	Barclays Agg 4.34%	Barclays Agg 2.43%	Barclays Agg 4.33%	Russell 2000 Value −9.78%	MSCI Emerging Markets −53.18%	Barclays Agg 5.93%	Barclays Agg 6.54%	MSCI Emerging Markets −18.17%	Barclays Agg 4.21%	MSCI Emerging Markets −2.27%

The Callan Periodic Table of Investment Returns conveys the strong *case for diversification* across asset classes (stocks vs. bonds), investment styles (growth vs. value), capitalizations (large vs. small), and equity markets (U.S. vs. international). The Table highlights the uncertainty inherent in all capital markets. Rankings change every year. Also noteworthy is the difference between absolute and relative performance, as returns for the top-performing asset class span a wide range over the past 20 years.

A printable copy of *The Callan Periodic Table of Investment Returns* is available on our website at **www.callan.com**

Callan | Knowledge. Experience. Integrity.

The Callan Periodic Table of Investment Returns 1994–2013

Callan's Periodic Table of Investment Returns depicts annual returns for 10 asset classes, ranked from best to worst performance for each calendar year. The asset classes are color-coded to enable easy tracking over time. We describe the well-known, industry-standard market indices that we use as proxies for each asset class in the text below.

● **Barclays Aggregate Bond Index** (formerly the Lehman Brothers Aggregate Bond Index) includes U.S. government, corporate, and mortgage-backed securities with maturities of at least one year.

● **Barclays Corporate High Yield Bond Index** measures the market of USD-denominated, non-investment grade, fixed-rate, taxable corporate bonds. Securities are classified as high yield if the middle rating of Moody's, Fitch, and S&P is Ba1/BB+/BB+ or below, excluding emerging market debt.

● **MSCI EAFE** is a Morgan Stanley Capital International Index that is designed to measure the performance of the developed stock markets of Europe, Australasia, and the Far East.

● **MSCI Emerging Markets** is a Morgan Stanley Capital International Index that is designed to measure the performance of equity markets in 21 emerging countries around the world.

Callan

Callan was founded as an employee-owned investment consulting firm in 1973. Ever since, we have empowered institutional clients with creative, customized investment solutions that are uniquely backed by proprietary research, exclusive data, ongoing education and decision support. Today, Callan advises on more than $1.8 trillion in total assets, which makes us among the largest independently owned investment consulting firms in the U.S. We use a client-focused consulting model to serve

● **Russell 2000** measures the performance of small capitalization U.S. stocks. The Russell 2000 is a market-value-weighted index of the 2,000 smallest stocks in the broad-market Russell 3000 Index. These securities are traded on the NYSE, AMEX, and NASDAQ.

● **Russell 2000 Value and** ● **Russell 2000 Growth** measure the performance of the growth and value styles of investing in small cap U.S. stocks. The indices are constructed by dividing the market capitalization of the Russell 2000 Index into Growth and Value indices, using style "factors" to make the assignment. The Value Index contains those Russell 2000 securities with a greater-than-average value orientation, while the Growth Index contains those securities with a greater-than-average growth orientation. Securities in the Value Index generally have lower price-to-book and price-earnings ratios than those in the Growth Index. The indices are market-capitalization-weighted. The constituent securities are not mutually exclusive.

● **S&P 500** measures the performance of large capitalization U.S. stocks. The S&P 500 is a market-value-weighted index of 500 stocks that are traded on the NYSE, AMEX, and NASDAQ. The weightings make each company's influence on the Index performance directly proportional to that company's market value.

● **S&P 500 Growth and** ● **S&P 500 Value** measure the performance of the growth and value styles of investing in large cap U.S. stocks. The indices are constructed by dividing the market capitalization of the S&P 500 Index into Growth and Value indices, using style "factors" to make the assignment. The Value Index contains those S&P 500 securities with a greater-than-average value orientation, while the Growth Index contains those securities with a greater-than-average growth orientation. The indices are market-capitalization-weighted. The constituent securities are not mutually exclusive.

Page 155

Many think that a great investment strategy is one that will "Beat the Market." But as you'll see when you read our final chapter, that's more often a losing strategy than a winning one.

Don't ignore human capital. Your ability to learn and grow and work is one of your biggest assets, especially when you are young. When making your financial Life Plan you will want to weigh how improving your credentials or skills will get you closer to your Life Plan, or take you further from it. Sometimes the wisest thing to invest in is yourself by getting a college degree or learning a new skill or maybe learning to write or play a musical instrument. At other times it can be a costly detour from achieving the life you want to live.

Don't ignore college expenses. The cost of college is increasing much faster than inflation. If you have children, you need a plan.

Much up-to-date information can be found on websites. For example, the Saving For College site, http://www.savingforcollege.com/ provides a "saving for college" tutorial that discusses some of the popular options such as 529 plans. The site helps you project and calculate costs and provides advice on many options. The College Board website http://www.collegeboard.com/student/pay/ provides information about how to apply for scholarships, loans, grants and other financial packages. It also provides college expense calculators and helps you estimate how much financial aid the student might get and how that will affect the net cost of college.

Discuss plans with your child well in advance of college. Talk about how much your child needs to work and save, how much she will need to borrow and what you can provide. Some students attend a good community college for two years to save money before transferring to a four-year college where they will earn their degree. Most high schools allow students to take college courses and earn college credit while they are still in high school.

Few parents will be able to foot the bill for college going forward. But your children will be able to get a college degree provided you plan in advance and work together.

3. *Taxes*

Taxes are a shadowy area for many of us. Nobody likes to pay them. America was founded on rebellion against taxation without representation. When someone prominent "cheats" on their taxes and gets caught it's big news. And it's an incredibly complex area of knowledge, with more in it than any single person can master.

A few things to keep in mind: It's not "corrupt" to take tax deductions. It is foolish not to. Tax deductions are there as part of the law of the land. They're there for your benefit. You should take advantage of every one you can. What is their value? Think of it this way. If you are in the 28% tax bracket, and your state tacks on another 5%, a tax deduction is worth 33% to you. That means whatever you buy that you then get to deduct on your tax return you're buying at a firesale! One third off the price. Where else can you get that kind of discount on what you buy? Take every deduction you are entitled to, and put the savings toward your Life Plan.

There are good books, encyclopedic in nature, written for consumers on taxes and deductions. You can find them online. As large as they are, they will miss many things an expert will catch. But if you're bent on doing your taxes yourself, get one of those books and study it. You may find that you can save yourself a bundle.

No matter what your age, your income or your goals, taxes will figure in your cash flow as well as in your investment choices. What you pay in taxes has a good deal to do with how much money is left to go toward your Life Plan or for you to save or spend. The less tax you pay, the more you have. Changes in the tax code in the last 15 years have vastly reduced the vehicles you can use to shelter money from taxes. The most popular remaining "shelter" is the money you invest in your home. That's because you are allowed to deduct the interest on your mortgage from your income every year before you pay taxes.

One of the significant advantages of investing in stocks or equities over CDs, bonds or money market is that long-term profits on stocks are taxed at reduced (capital gains) rates, while interest income is taxed at the higher ordinary income tax rate. Financial advisers will consider the tax implications of any financial moves you might make. But good planners say: "Don't let the tax tail wag the dog," which simply means that while you will want to consider tax implications, other goals for investments should be given priority over tax strategies.

Here are some tax definitions that may help you as you consider investment vehicles:

- Tax advantaged is a catchall term that can be used to describe practically any kind of investment including those bulleted below. It means nothing specific.

- Tax deferred means that current taxes are not due on an investment. Annuities, some retirement plans and the cash value on life insurance policies enjoy tax deferral on investment earnings. Taxes are not due until the money is withdrawn.

- Tax free means that no taxes are due ever on an investment. That is the case for some types of bonds issued by federal and state governments. Municipal bonds, which are issued by state, city, or other local governments to pay for projects, are free of federal taxes. Often called "munis," many of these bonds are also free of state and local taxes.

- Pretax means that you may use money for some purchase before you pay taxes on it. That's the case with money you are permitted to spend for certain health care needs. When you contribute to a 401(k) plan, you use pretax dollars. That money is subtracted from the compensation on which you pay tax that year. So if you earn $75,000 and put $5,000 into a 401(k) plan, your income will be reported as $70,000. Suppose your combined federal and state tax bracket is 35%. If you took your $5,000 as taxable income, you would pay $1,750 in federal and state taxes, leaving you $3,250 to spend. When you contribute to the 401(k) plan instead, you put the full $5,000 into your retirement account. Your 401(k) also gives you continued tax deferral – or postponement of taxes – on both the money you contribute and the investment earnings on that money until you withdraw money from the plan.

4. *Retirement*

Retirement has changed a good deal in the last few decades. Your working life and your retirement life are not two distinct phases, one drudgery and one pleasure. Those who plan successfully knit the two together, almost seamlessly. Of course, this requires a good deal of thought – about who you are, what you want, what you enjoy, where you're going. To me, one of the most important aspects of Life Planning is that it helps you plan for your whole life, so that you are following your passion during your work life as well as into retirement.

We've talked about the importance of Social Security income for your BERT analysis. Even more important for many of us is the amount we have contributed to our own individual retirement accounts, including our IRA's. Most retirement plans are tax advantaged, usually meaning that you pay no taxes while the fund is accumulating gains year after year. Wherever there's a tax advantage, there's some free money available for your Life Plan and it's worthwhile knowing your options here. It's also worth exploring what percentage of your savings should go into a tax-advantaged retirement account versus into a saving or investment account. Your ordinary savings can provide you flexibility before your retirement age, whereas your retirement accounts can grow more rapidly and tax advantaged for your retirement years. As we've suggested, if you can get a free or matching employer contribution to a 401(k) program it is advisable to take it.

For more information on retirement savings, see:

*   http://www.smartmoney.com/invest/strategies/how-to-invest-for-retirement-1304670365583/

Pensions

If you retire from an employer after a long career, you will probably get some kind of pension. A traditional pension is called a "defined benefit plan," because it defines the annual pension benefit you receive. It is designed to reward loyal employees who spent their entire careers with one company. The benefit is heavily weighted toward the later working years when the employee's salary is the highest. A good plan should replace about 50% of income for an employee with 30 years' service. But few retirees today have spent their careers at a single employer.

The benefit from a traditional pension is calculated as a percent of your final salary times years of service with the company. A typical plan might provide 1.2% to 1.5% of the average of your final three years of compensation times your years of service as an annual pension. Suppose you earn $100,000 a year. So 1.5% of that is $1,500. If you have been with the company for 40 years, you will get a pension benefit of $60,000 a year in retirement. Work 25 years and you earn $37,500; five years, $7,500. So job hopping, as most of us do today, results in very low – if any – pension benefit. The 401(k) plan or "defined contribution" plan has been set up to shift the responsibility for saving for retirement to employees, who must put their own money aside, probably with some kind of match from the employer. If you retire with a pension benefit, you will likely be given two options: Take the pension in a guaranteed annual payment for the rest of your life or take it as a single lump sum. If you take the lump sum, the employer is shifting the market and mortality risks to you. If you are offered a substantial lump sum after a long career, you should consider professional advice on how to invest it to last for your lifetime. See our chapter on finding a financial adviser you can trust.

You will still need to decide when to begin taking social security benefits. There has been much debate over the years about whether to register for social security benefits at age 62, when you will receive a partial benefit, or to wait. Changes in social security benefits and retirement ages have altered the possible answers to these questions, but the biggest factor is your expected longevity. If you can afford to wait, and you expect to live well beyond average, you will not want to collect benefits till you can collect the maximum at age 70.

Workers born in 1937 or before earn full benefits at age 65. If they decide to take benefits at age 62, the earliest age permissible, those benefits are reduced by 20% permanently. So if your earned benefit is $1,000 at full retirement age, and you begin collecting $800 at age 62, the $800, plus cost of living adjustments, is what you will receive for the rest of your life. The age for full retirement, "normal retirement," is increasing. For those born between 1946 and 1954, normal retirement age is 66. You can still begin receiving benefits at age 62, but the reduction in benefits is increased to 25% so in our example above, you would receive $750 in benefits for the rest of your life. On the other hand if you wait four years to begin to collect at 70, your benefit will increase by 32% or 8% per year. The normal retirement age continues to creep up each month until it reaches 67 for those born in 1960 and later.

5. *Estate Planning and Inheritances*

Although we should never count on them, unless trusts are already funded, it can be very helpful to know the inheritance you will receive. I encourage you to find the right time and place to have a conversation with your parents about their intentions. Additionally, to protect the legacy aspects of your Life Plan, you will want a will and an estate plan. I would consult a professional for both. If you don't have a will, the laws of the state where you reside will determine what happens to your estate (and your young children!), rather than your wishes.

A website I recommend www.yourafterlife.com is a great place to begin thinking about these issues. It also provides a marvelous space for a secure and lasting digital version of what's important to you. It provides you with a way of putting your personal legacy online, digitally, so that it might be there for generations to come. This can mean a tremendous amount for your loved ones and provide a rich family link into history for your descendents. We are all used to wills and legacies being left with physical objects. In this digital age we can leave a record of everything we love online. The website is a social media site, and you can pick and choose both what you share and who you share it with. I've begun to put things on it myself and feel I'm only scratching the surface of its potential as I post favorite memories, a timeline of my life, a biography, pictures, books etc. Even practical issues regarding your will, your funeral, inheritances and instructions for your executor can be designed on the site. It's a secure ad-free online platform that ensures the safety and availability of your data into eternity.

In Conclusion

The moments of seeing your financial plan in place and knowing that your Life Plan is secure are thrilling moments. As much so as crafting the Vision in the first place, and solving the Obstacles. They bring us to the next chapter and to the final phase of EVOKE® that we call Execution.

Execution - EVOKE®
Bringing Our Brilliance to Life
(and Signing Some Documents Along the Way)

Perhaps the most important thing in our life is accomplishing what we were born to do, being the person we were meant to be, expressing ourselves in the world and to our loved ones with all the authenticity that makes us who we are. We each are born with a share of light to deliver to the world, a light the world needs us to shine as brilliantly as we can. Personally I can think of nothing more important. It's a tragedy if we don't. It's why in Execution, the accomplishment of our Life Plans is so important.

Have you ever known someone who died before their prime, someone perhaps just coming into their own, someone with gifts inside them they were just becoming aware of, someone perhaps who had put off an authentic life for years, someone you loved?

I have. He was one of the most remarkable clients I ever had, and at times one of the strangest, certainly one of the most infuriating. He was the only person in my long career whom I nearly threw out of my office – twice! Richard had left himself out of his life somehow. I'm not sure without Life Planning that he ever would have fully lived.

Our first meeting was not auspicious. When Richard walked into my office I recognized him, and was taken aback. Why would one of the best-known mutual fund and hedge fund managers in Boston be coming to see me? I was even more surprised when I glanced at his net worth. Not terrible, but nowhere near what one would expect from a star manager.

"I'm not here to invest with you, George. Both of us know how I ought to be doing that. I'm here for another reason." His statement was strong, but his affect was odd. He was constantly looking about him; his head leaned to one side. I'm one of those fellows who prides himself on being able to size up a person in the first minutes of a meeting, but I was totally perplexed both by his manner and his statement. My first thought, as I glanced at his net worth, was "I wonder if this fellow is a gambler." And my second thought was "Uh oh," knowing how challenging it could be to give up such a habit, and worrying a bit already about his expectations of me. It did nothing to allay my concern that he didn't want my investment expertise, something I particularly prided myself upon and had built my business around.

"Nope," he said, "I want something else from you." He mumbled inaudibly, looked out the window, fumbled with his fingers, made some incidental remarks about my décor and office in Harvard Square. All the while, I'm thinking, well, get on with it then. Let's hear it. Why are you here? But I said nothing, giving him the space to get there in his own way. Odd he might be, but no one could question his sense of purpose.

"I've never been able to invest my own money," he finally blurted out.

"Huh?"

"No, I've invested all these years for other people. All kinds of stocks, I've used hedges and options. Never been able to invest for myself."

I glanced once again at his net worth, this time noticing that everything he owned was in cash. I think when I first saw it I just assumed that it was a strategic move on his part, a short-term concern about the economy. I even wondered with a touch of envy, given his reputation for brilliance, if I should be doing something similar.

"That's right. What you see there is how it's always been. I'm ashamed of it. It makes me want to throw up. I feel like I have no integrity. For decades I've invested for other people, made good money for them, but I've never been able to do it for myself. Can't put my money where my mouth is."

"What?" and for a moment I lost my cool, all my preaching about empathy out the window. "You've got to be kidding me?"

"Nope, that's the real thing, George. God knows I've tried. Many an evening coming home from work, I'm in agony about it. Have been for years. Nobody knows. You're the first person I've told. I've been carrying this with me for over 20 years."

His odd mannerisms, his strange and constant twisting of tissues, his rapid looking about, his awkward pushing of the conversation all began to make sense. This extraordinarily successful man had no way of feeling his success and was finding ways to sabotage it. Instead he felt like he'd been carrying a lie for 20 years, living it secretly. I'd rarely been in the presence of someone so deeply troubled by a secret life.

"So why do you want to see me?" I asked.

"You're going to fix it," he responded. I don't know why but suddenly I had this image of myself as Eliot Ness or Wyatt Earp, and I didn't feel comfortable at all about the role that he was putting me in.

"Look Richard, this is deep stuff you are talking about. It's not in my terrain. I don't know how to fix it." And I then did something I don't think I'd ever done before and have only done a few times since. "You know I think you need someone to really listen to you, to how awful this has been, someone who can empathize and has listened to things like this many times before. I think you need to speak to a psychologist." I reached for my Rolodex. "And I know several people personally, really wonderful human beings, whom I've known for years who I could refer you to." I pulled out three cards.

"You're not listening, George. I'm here to see you. I'm rather desperate about this. You're going to fix it. That's why I'm here. Do you understand?"

The truth is I was a bit frightened at this point. I thought the fellow could be truly crazy and I was beginning to plot how I could get him out of my office.

"You've written about me George. I've read your writings." He pulled out a sheaf of papers and waved them at me. "This is about money," he said. "I won't go to those other people. You can fix this. I'm not saying I'll be easy, but

I'd run circles around those other people. You get it. You understand money and you understand people. You're the only one that can help me make this happen and I'm determined that we do this, we do this together. I can't live like this anymore."

Richard was beginning to affect me. I was beginning to understand, and even believe him that he wouldn't let anyone else near the problem. His shame was too great, and the potential for being misunderstood. I had been concerned that he was expecting too much from me. That it was a setup for failure, my failure at the very least. But when he shifted to talking about how "we" could do the work, and how determined he was to change himself, I knew we had a chance to do quite a piece of work together.

"So Richard, if we are to do this, I have two ground rules. One is that we meet every week, schedules permitting, until you are fully invested in a balanced portfolio. The second is that you do the homework assignments I come up with each week to further you toward your goal. Are you game?"

"That's why I've come to see you. I was hoping you'd say that."

Among the assignments I gave him over the next several weeks were the exercises you have accomplished already, as you have read this book. His Third Question had a few other elements in it besides investing, but he was emphatic, none of those other things could be accomplished until this one task was completed. He could take no pleasure in anything, until this wound was healed. There could be no Torch of a traditional kind unless we dealt with this monster.

So we went at it with abandon. The work we did was deep, largely internal and contemplative, practices I've written about in Transforming Suffering into Wisdom *(2006), and in the Understanding chapter of* Seven Stages of Money Maturity *(1999). Richard was learning to be more at ease in his feelings, less attached to his thoughts and not so preoccupied with himself. There was no question he was a smart fellow. In fact he was quite competitive about even these skills. It was as if he wanted to show me just how smart he could be. He learned surprisingly quickly to come to a more peaceful place when he felt anxiety or shame or guilt, and the thoughts they accompanied pulled him toward inappropriate actions. He became similarly successful when his habitual patterns of behavior kept him from acting in ways he knew were dignified and correct. Not that he was perfect at it. He didn't need to be. Just good enough to accomplish his mission.*

Externally, we drove toward action. Much of what he learned came from the Vigor chapter of Seven Stages. I did not know Prochaska's Changing for Good *(1995) at that time, but I intuitively worked from many of his principles. Prochaska's work more than any other addresses the drive necessary to overcome bad habits and how to access it. Slowly but steadily we moved together through Prochaska's stages from contemplation to preparation to action and finally to maintenance, all described quite clearly although in relation to drinking and smoking, in Prochaska's book.*

It took a little over eight weeks, somewhere between six and eight meetings. A very unusual situation, outside the normal structure of EVOKE® and unlike any I'd ever been involved with. I wouldn't be sharing this story with you except that it illustrates how important it is that we address and accomplish, execute upon, our Third Question and our Torch. Without those things being accomplished, some part of our own lives is like Richard's.

One Friday at the end of our eight week period, Richard surprised me by showing up in my office unannounced. He said he'd been in Harvard Square, and just wanted to share with me two extraordinary changes in his life, just happening, that he felt I was responsible for his accomplishing. By this point I had grown quite fond of him, amazed at the rapidity of his transformation and was happy to see his sense of informal freedom in this visit, not to mention his wish to share with me his joy.

"I've done it George, I've done it!" he said with extraordinary energy and glee. "I'm invested. Every dime of it. It's done."

"Wow, Richard, how wonderful! I'm so happy for you. Incredible."

"Yep, I did it all myself, right to the penny the asset allocation we'd discussed. I started to do a dollar-cost averaging approach, and then thought, nope, this is permanent money, long term. If I just start putting in dribs and drabs, I may chicken out. So here goes! And off it went."

"Well that's wonderful, Richard. You must feel really satisfied."

"I sure do. And you know what? It's already begun to shift how I am in the rest of my life. In fact that's the second surprise I wanted to tell you. This weekend I'm going to break up with my girlfriend."

"What?"

"Yeah, we've never been able to talk about things. I'm not sure she's right for me George, and we've just kind of been dragging the thing on for the past eight years, and I've just decided I'm going to move out."

"Pardon me, Richard, I'm confused."

"I know we never really talked about this."

"Richard, let me get this straight. You've been living with your girlfriend for eight years and you're going to walk out on her this weekend?"

"Yeah, we just don't communicate."

"Well have you talked with her about this?"

"About what?"

"About moving out, and not communicating well. Have you tried to talk this through with her? Have you tried to fix this?"

"God no, George. That would hurt her too much."

"And walking out won't hurt her? What are you talking about Richard? Who is it that can't bear the pain? Is it her or is it you? You've been learning over the past few months how to be more at ease with your anxieties, well why don't you try to practice it with her? Feel your own feelings, man, and talk to her about your differences. See what happens."

"No George, you don't understand"

"Don't understand! You've got to be kidding me. You're going to walk out on a woman who's loved you and lived with you for eight years without first trying to make things better? And you're telling me I don't understand. Where's your understanding, man? You can just get out of my office, Richard. You haven't learned a thing in all the weeks I've been working with you. If you don't have the courtesy or the courage to talk with her about what you don't like in the relationship, please just go!"

Richard was just as heated as I was. He grabbed his hat from the chair with both a gesture and a groan of disgust, and walked with passion out of my space.

We'd had an appointment scheduled for the end of the following week. I didn't know what to expect, but he showed up, a little sheepish, but a grin on his face. He'd gone home that night and had a long talk with his girlfriend, "the best talk we ever had. In fact we just kept talking all weekend long. It was as if we had fallen in love again. Every once in a while, over the years, she's hinted at how it might be nice if we got married someday, well Sunday night we went out to Aujourdui, and I proposed." He paused. "She accepted."

Our mission together was now pretty well accomplished. I felt privileged to keep up with Richard over the next few years. I got to know his children from a prior marriage, and to see that his whole family life was thriving.

We also came to share a spiritual community together in Cambridge, and I was amazed once again at how quickly he became a leader there, speaking with authority, depth and passion. What impressed me the most was how clearly he spoke about issues of ethics, responsibility and morality. He always spoke with kindness. He never judged another, but his insights were so pure he could reach right through a complex dilemma to where a person would be genuinely inspired to do the right thing, to be a fine person, to model it, to change their lives. He reached out and touched people from every walk of life. In fact, he was much more naturally close to those who had nothing, than to those who had been materially successful. He became a mentor, someone without question whom you could trust, someone you would go to if you were in trouble. I don't think he ever lost the sense that I was his teacher, but the truth is he taught me something in every encounter, starting with the very first time we met. He kept teaching me how to be better than I was. I think that's the gift he learned to give to everyone.

There's one thing I forgot to mention. At the heart of his Torch there were three things. We've covered two of them. Straightening out his integrity around his personal investing, his family and relationships. The third was a kind of image of the sense of freedom that he wanted and had held himself back from. He wanted to get on a motorcycle and just ride, completely free, from one end of the country to the other. He didn't even have a motorcycle, and always felt tied to the daily fluctuations of investment markets, so he'd never come close to realizing this dream. But we got him a motorcycle, and within a year he was off on a long, long ride.

One afternoon, I remember it was the middle of the week, I was pushing papers at my office and I got a call from Richard. I thought he might be setting up an appointment, but I could hear the wind in the phone he was calling from, somewhere in the midwest I think. He said he'd been riding along and was struck by lightning kind of, had dropped his bike and had to call me. "Listen George, I just want you to know, I've done everything. I've got everything. Everything I ever wanted in all my life. I'm a free man. I just wanted you to know because you did it. I've never been so happy in all my life. If I were to die tomorrow I would have no regrets, no more mountains to climb, I would die in peace."

Late the next year I learned that Richard had been struck with a very rapidly moving brain cancer, had lost much of his ability to get around and to speak. As soon as I heard, I let the family know they could count on me for anything they might need. It was sometime around Christmas I got a call from them. I don't remember now if it was from his wife or one of his daughters, but they were all together. They all knew this was the end. "Within a few hours, I expect," she said. "I wouldn't have bothered you, but it was Richard's last request, to talk with you. He can't really talk, but I know he'd like to hear your voice."

Richard's path wasn't an easy one, but none of our paths are. He came to a point in his life where he simply knew he had to do things differently, where he had to live the life of freedom that he had actually glimpsed in childhood. I was lucky to know him.

In Life Planning, most of us come to that same point in our lives. It's usually when we confront the Third Question and recognize that our life is slipping away without the most critical things being accomplished. Within just a few years, Richard accomplished the three ideals of his Third Question, and knew beyond a shadow of a doubt that he was free.

Life Planning sets us free. Often we think of Execution as an interview where we sign documents, fund our retirement, purchase the necessary insurance. But it is also the stage of EVOKE® where we ride our motorcycle across the windy plains of the midwest, where we fall in love again and marry the woman or man of our dreams, where we confront a gaping hole in our own integrity and overcome it.

Louis' Story

The last I heard from Louis, Anita was enjoying her new work immensely. She had not yet managed to make it a financial success, but it wasn't a burden. More of her Life Plan was coming true from Ben's success. Together they were planning a family "vacation" in China. For Ben, of course, China would involve some work, but his excitement continued. He felt he had found his calling, and was greatly enjoying studying Chinese with Anita in their evenings as they prepared for the trip.

The Execution phase of EVOKE® with a Life Planner can take place inside or outside a meeting, or in between meetings. It is the time of action or the accounting of actions taken. More often than not, by the time Execution rolls around, many of the life dreams of the client have already been acted on and even accomplished, but there are often many significant ones remaining, and usually a number of financial actions that still need to happen coming out of the Knowledge and financial planning meeting. Often there is insurance that needs to be purchased, retirement plans that need to be funded, assets rearranged or put in order. The Execution meeting can thus be a meeting where forms are prepared for signing, or a meeting where action steps are reported upon and follow-up steps recommended, or a review meeting that also celebrates all of the accomplishments to date. Some advisers and clients use it to insure accountability on the actions required for the Life Plan to be fully lived and fully funded.

In other words, Execution isn't merely signing off on documents and buying insurance or funding retirement. In Life Planning, execution means taking that extra time to go swimming with your son, to take your daughter on a special trip, to begin to heal the wounds with your parents, to take pride in the practice of the guitar and the songs that you are creating, to start the new business, to notice each time you fail to bring kindness or patience into your relationships and to feel the vitality, warmth and rich connections that come when you succeed.

Life Plans Accomplished

Here are some examples of Life Plans accomplished:

Let's start with another sailing story. John was depressed and bored with his life when he first encountered a financial Life Planner. One of the shocking things revealed in their first meeting was a decade-long addiction to drugs that matched, he felt, a decade of working jobs he couldn't stand. John hadn't sailed since he was seven or eight years old, but in his Third Question he dreamed of sailing around the world. Charles, the financial planner, had sailed around the world several times and let John know he could achieve his dream, but there was work to do! John was so inspired at the thought of living a life of his own choosing, he challenged himself to end his addiction, spent months with a therapist and dedicated many hours a week getting in shape so that he could be relied upon as part of a ship's crew. In fact he lost 20% of his body weight and eight months later Charles got a call from him in San Francisco celebrating the first leg of his trip. "I feel free," John said. "I don't know how else to describe it. Thank you."

Marieke came to Life Planning inspired by the belief that the world was on the verge of environmental sustainability. She wanted to find a way to contribute to that movement. She hoped Life Planning would make her role in it clear. But during the Exploration phase, and in her Three Questions, something surprising appeared, something that had so much negative energy that it took over her Life Plan and became an obstacle that she had to solve before she could do any good for the world. Marieke had a best friend from childhood. They had been there for each other at every stage of their lives. They had been each other's maid of honor at their weddings, they were the godmothers of each other's children. But six months ago, they had fought and said things to one another that were extremely hurtful. They had stopped their daily chatting and had no contact since then—not even a birthday card. Marieke felt hurt, sad, depressed. At some point every day the thought of it would overwhelm her and all her vigor and joy would drain out. She said in the Exploration meeting, "I cannot imagine moving forward on this greatest adventure of my life without her beside me." She knew it was going to take more than just one call or visit to patch it up, so she made the first stage of her Execution all about working carefully to reconcile and rebuild this crucial relationship. Three months later, she came back with joy and more energy than she had ever felt in her life, and was able to launch into her passion with abandon.

Marjorie and Tom were trained as architects. Tom had an enriching, creative life, doing residential architecture and working in his own business where he specialized in building one-of-a-kind unique properties for individuals. He was an excellent architect and got great satisfaction from completing projects and seeing the client's delight with his work. Marjorie, however, was unhappy. She had left architecture and gone into accounting where she earned much more than her husband, but she felt stifled and unfulfilled. Life Planning brought her passion back. After working with her Life Planner, Dan Boyce, Marjorie left her accounting job, became more actively connected with Tom's work and started getting more involved in community work. "She's quite a different person now," Dan said. "Relaxed and happy."

Anja Luesink, an RLP® in New York City was visited by a young woman working in a law office with lots of overtime. She had come in with reams of financial papers, but hadn't answered any of the Life Planning questions Anja had sent to her. She hadn't seen their relevance in a financial meeting. Anja wasn't sure what to do. Unhappy and confused, her client had many conflicting and even overwhelming financial objectives. It was easy to imagine a life burdened by constant financial issues and concerns. When Anja decided to ask the Life Planning questions in person, her client was surprised but quickly settled in to describe how much she longed to work less, have time to travel, learn languages and in a few years become a travel writer. She thanked Anja profusely, as she had never put this all together for herself before, and before their meetings were finished she had a concrete plan to accomplish her dreams. Within months Anja was receiving postcards from Korea, China and Japan.

Jim lost his wife when he was 55; she was 50. He worked as an engineer and disliked it greatly. Distraught and confused he sought out a Registered Life Planner®. It was the right decision. Discovering he had adequate funds to take the risk, he cut back at work to address the centerpiece of his Third Question, a deep regret that he didn't pursue the photography work he'd excelled at in college and high school. Over time it became more his profession than engineering, although he always said he brought his engineering mind to his photography. He became quite well regarded, had a unique style and loved to teach. It was in one of his classes that he met his wife to be, but that is yet another story and another passion.

Lois worked at the same medical lab for her entire career. When she turned 60, she panicked, terrified to face the possibility of retiring. She lived alone and felt she had no interests outside work. Her life was comfortable, even if it was not quite fulfilling. She felt both afraid and overcome with inertia. What surprised her when she did Life Planning was how many interests she really had but had never pursued. She began volunteering in charitable programmes and started what she calls her "second career" in community theatre playing musical roles and helping the theatre secure a stronger place in community life. "I never imagined life could be so much fun," she told her planner. She wasn't afraid of retirement at all.

When Ellen and Nigel came in to see Justin King, RLP®, everything seemed to be going wrong. They felt they were scrambling just to get by. Their lives were scattered in all directions and they felt as if nothing ever got done. Truth was, nothing was getting done on what was truly important to them. That was revealed in their Third Question where they listed very specific regrets – not having a child, not publishing a book, not being able to relieve the tension in a family business. Life Planning brought focus to their lives and filled them with drive and vitality. The couple sent a huge thank you card to Justin. "We were both blown away by our work with you. Now we look at our future in such a bright way." When Justin checked in with them later, Ellen had had her book published and was pregnant with twins. Nigel had grown more relaxed at work and from the focus he had gathered with Justin, the bulk of his financial burdens had been lifted.

Holly, 58, who had an asset management business, took the EVOKE® training program because she wanted to answer some questions in her own life. What came out of her work was the realization that she and her husband felt passionate about living in Mexico and wanted to spend more time there. Within two years, both gave up their businesses, (her husband was a photographer). In exchange they bought a number of acres on the Sea of Cortez in Mexico and settled in a village two hours north of Puerto Vallarta. They are now building a community and an infrastructure to sustain the economy in their little fishing village, where fishing seems to become more difficult every day. They are also putting in an internet café and other services to help the townspeople to modernize. "The cost of living is much lower there," says Dan Boyce, RLP® and Holly's partner in the Kinder workshop. "She is living the life of her dreams."

Lars came to Life Planning with his wife, Tessa. He told his Life Planner that he would be an easy case, because he loved his job, he loved his wife and family, and there was nothing he would change. His First and Second Questions reflected that. He said in essence that he wouldn't change a thing. But then he came to the Third Question. He really imagined himself on the verge of death, and terror filled him, followed by unbearable grief. He had a perfect life, but he would have to leave it behind when he died, and then what? What would his life have amounted to, and what would be its meaning, and what, if anything, survived the grave? Lars saw that while the surface of his life was a dream, lurking beneath it was a void that felt to him like a nightmare. Yet he did not believe that. The love he experienced in his life convinced him that there must be some light, some loving spiritual presence that went far beneath the surface of life and that survived beyond death. Much to his surprise, his Life Plan became the start of an intentional spiritual journey – something he had never had any interest in before. His Execution opened to him unsuspected depths of life and love that he found through reading and attending retreats and eventually becoming part of a spiritual community. He came into Life Planning thinking he could not be any happier or more content, but his happiness matured over the next few years into joy, and his contentment matured into peace. He continues to thank his Life Planner, saying how with Life Planning's help his suffering in that moment of despair at death in the Third Question led him to wisdom and gifts he did not even know he was missing.

When Charles Robertson attended the 5-Day workshop to become a Registered Life Planner®, his own life turned around. "I'd never been to a retreat before, never been to a dry hotel and definitely never meditated," he said. "I went with a completely open mind," he said. "That week, my life changed. I realized I'd been missing in some way my sense of purpose, and I rediscovered it there." Part of Charles' execution was to bring music back into his life. He is singing again and regularly attends mass at Westminster Cathedral.

Zach was a school teacher but had come to hate his work. When he went to Life Planner Phil Dyer to go through the EVOKE® process with his wife, Marilee, he was burned out, disliked D.C. and he was worried about making a connection with his one-year-old son. Zach, Marilee and Phil worked out a plan for a one-year sabbatical for them to explore who they really were and who they wanted to be. Their house in D.C. attracted a bidding war and they sold it in two days. The couple got a year's lease on a place in Maine with instructions from Phil to just chill out for three months. "Don't set an agenda," Phil said. "Explore who you want to be going forward. Call or email me immediately with any insights." That time changed their lives.

Dale, 51, came to Tom Greider, a Life Planner in Oregon because he had become burned out in the insurance industry after 25 plus years. He had reached a point in his life where he realized he was not having the impact with coaching and mentoring kids that he truly desired. His love for baseball, the outdoors, fishing, hiking, writing, were all taking a backseat to the daily grind of running a family business that was draining the vigor and passion from his life. He quit the business cold turkey. Now, he needed to know, what's next, how could he accomplish these dreams and aspirations, and still provide for his family? By going through the EVOKE® process with Tom, Dale discovered that he could return to coaching high school baseball, devote more time to his writings, hike the Pacific Crest Trail, and pursue his true passion of helping and inspiring others, especially kids. He started his own river guide business, and currently takes kids and their families on excursions that allow Dale to share his passions with those in his community.

Gary Witten is a Registered Life Planner®. What makes him so good is the personal passion that was rekindled in his own life from being Life Planned. It transformed both his life and his marriage. He was a self-described workaholic on a treadmill, filling his life with meaningless things. The Three Questions changed everything. He made significant changes in his life and achieved success in his business by dramatically cutting the meaningless hours he was spending there – cutting many days a month. Revivified in his personal life as well as in his relationships with his wife and son, Gary's passion for Life Planning brought hundreds of clients to its benefits. Through his great vitality and generosity he has shared with other advisers around the world the structure of his seminars and PowerPoint presentations that have been so successful.

For me, completing Life Planning for You is part of the Execution phase of my Life Plan. For years I've wanted to write a sequel to *The Seven Stages of Money Maturity* (1999). I've wanted to write a book that in some way would complete what I had to say to consumers of financial services and to the general public. Much of that has now been accomplished.

Self-Help and Moving On

What remains on your Life Plan to be done? What action steps remain on your Goals for Your Life for you to take? It's time to live our Life Plans, time to make them happen.

You have become the greatest expert on your own life. You know what you need to do to fulfill your highest purpose and meaning in life. If you are working on your own without a Life Planner, the biggest challenge you now have is holding yourself accountable to your Plan. I suggest you make a habit of reading your Torch at the start and end of every day. In the morning, take a few minutes to reflect on what you can do today to make it burn a little more brightly, to fulfill it a little more than yesterday. In the evening, write down what you did that was truest to your vision and filled you with joy, and what happened that felt like the opposite direction and drained your vigor. Reflect on how tomorrow can have more of the joy and less of the drain. Once a week, set aside an hour to look at your obstacles and solutions and make a plan to move forward on whatever feels most promising to your vision's fulfillment. It would also be helpful to have a partner to meet with monthly – a spouse or friend, for instance – to whom you are accountable for executing your plan.

For those of you who want the many benefits of an experienced guide to walk with you on the exciting journey of your plan's Execution, I hope in the next chapter, to inspire you to find someone who will work brilliantly with you. I know for most of us there is a cloud that hangs over the financial services industry in general and financial advisers in particular. As I describe how to find a financial adviser you can trust, I invite you to think carefully with me how you would like the financial industry and its professions to be in the future, so that they will never betray your confidence again, so that they will be of genuine service to you, your children and to people of every walk of life all over the world for years to come. I personally aspire for this profession to be one that all of us would want to join or for our children to join, not because of money, but because it has become the profession above all others that models integrity and delivers freedom into the lives of all human beings. I hope you will enjoy this next chapter that addresses both what financial services has been and what it is destined to become.

The Ideal Financial Adviser
&
How To Find One

Introduction

What makes a great financial adviser?

A great financial adviser is dedicated to putting your life together around money. They don't just help you invest and they're certainly not a salesperson. Trouble is they are hard to find. Each of us would be more successful, more at ease, happier and more vital knowing that our money-life was put together to deliver the life we most want to live.

As a boy I began to form a vision of what great financial advice meant. When I delivered the *Martins Ferry Times Leader* in St. Clairsville, Ohio, I particularly enjoyed Saturday mornings when I would awake long before anyone else in town. With each solitary step my imagination would wander and I sometimes pondered the personal devastation that would come if I were to lose my parents and have to fend for myself. What would I do? Did my parents have savings? Perhaps. Would I have to sell the house and live on the proceeds? Who could help me? Image from Merrill Lynch TV ads immediately came to mind: the symbol and model of financial probity, of caring, of a force for the good charging like a bull, yet stopping to listen to whomever came in, ready and able to help in all ways financial, with comprehensive financial knowledge and compassion, great listening skills, integrity, and best of all, with the vision to understand how to help me achieve what I wanted from life and to show me how it could best be delivered.

How innocent that boyhood dream, considering the ravages of the banking crisis we've just come through and the culpability of so many of our large financial companies. How badly we now need a financial services industry that models integrity in its actions and delivers freedom to its customers. Let me be among the first to break through the cynicism and argue that this dream is actually here. Already there are advisers who practice this way and whom we can find in searchable databases of financial advisers all over the world. Everyday these databases grow larger, with people we can trust.

Here I will show you how to find the very best of them. Moreover I fully expect a great financial services firm to arrive branded and recognizable, like a Starbucks, an iPhone (or even a Merrill!), in the next decade. Why? Because all of the constituent elements are already here, and because the consumer wants nothing less. In a genuinely free market system, consumers always win. They will win this as well.

The Primary Objectives: Trust & Freedom

More than anything else, the financial adviser you choose must be able to deliver two things. They must be someone you can trust and someone who can, through a combination of great listening skills and exceptional financial skills, deliver the freedoms you desire into your life. As you search for an adviser, you will be asking yourself:

- Does the adviser and the system he or she works under have unquestionable integrity? Can I trust them?

- And do they have the capacity, the experience, the dedication and the training to deliver the freedom I need to bring my very best into the world and into the community around me?

Trust and Freedom are different but overlapping issues.
For *Trust* and *Integrity* you will be investigating:

- Does the adviser swear to a fiduciary standard in their relationship with you, and what is the quality of their fiduciary obligations? Fiduciary is a legal term obligating a person to act solely on behalf of the person they are representing and in good faith.

- Are there conflicts of interest in how the adviser charges you? Are there more with one than with another adviser you might work with? Is it possible to eliminate them? Minimize them?

- Do they hold the requisite professional designations for the kind of work you will be expecting?

- Are they trained in relationship skills? Is that evident when you meet them in the way they listen to you, how they make it your meeting, not theirs? And when they do speak, can you clearly understand what they are telling you or do you feel mystified or patronized? Do you have a sense that they believe in you, or simply in their own products and analyses?

- Have there been formal actions taken against them or their firm?

- In a crisis, would they be one of the first persons you would want to turn to? Would they be available?

For *Freedom* and their ability to deliver it, you will be asking some overlapping questions but with a difference:

- Are they trained in the relationship skills that will help you to identify and elaborate upon what you care most about?

- Are they great communicators, and much more important, are they great listeners?

- Are they dedicated to your dream of freedom, about what you want most in life? You should be able to ascertain this from your very first meeting. Do they have the personal capacity and commitment to not merely support you, but on occasion remind and inspire you about the dreams you hold most dear? In that first meeting do you feel excited about your dreams, without hesitancy?

- Is it clear that their primary purpose is not to deliver you to their financial products or advice but to deliver freedom into your life? If it isn't, look for someone else.

- Do they have the financial designations and skills to identify the clearest, quickest and simplest path to your objectives?

- Do they have the best of the *comprehensive* financial planning designations so that they will not ignore one financial avenue in favor of another they are trained in or paid by?

- Are their fees and the fees of their recommended investments modest enough that you feel confident they will deliver to you more value than they will cost, both in their investment choices, and elsewhere?

- Do their investment criteria meet your own?

The Six Overriding Fallacies of Choosing a Financial Adviser

We all have false ideas about finances that get us into trouble. Six that appear harmless and yet have caused great suffering for many people are:

1. The Financial Adviser Fallacy

2. The "Why Should You Care about Fees, It's the Returns that Matter?" Fallacy

3. The Large Institution Fallacy

4. The Active Investing Fallacy (or the Advantages of Passive Investing)

5. The Best Friend Fallacy

6. The Do-It-Yourself or the News/Advice Fallacy

1. *The Financial Adviser Fallacy*

You can expect there to be some great money gurus in any listing of financial advisers, but it's akin to searching for the needle in the haystack. The *odds are stacked heavily against you finding them.* Here is why.

Initially, independent advisers, not affiliated with large companies, used the term financial adviser to distinguish their work of advice from the sales focus of stock brokers, but without a standard designation the term never meant much. It meant even less as the large financial services companies appropriated the label for their brokerage community, that is, for their "salespeople," who often aren't advisers at all. Brokers earn money by selling products and receiving commissions, just like car salesmen. The problem is there is always a conflict of interest because they must decide whether you get the best and cheapest product or they – and the brokerages – get the biggest commission. The consumers, of course, assumed they were getting investment advice, but those "advisers" were simply salespeople, selling product, with no fiduciary responsibilities whatsoever. This continues to mislead consumers.

The Fiduciary Standard

The Investment Adviser Act of 1940 requires an adviser to act as a fiduciary for clients, which means the client's best interest always comes first. That's the standard for an investment adviser, but a mere financial adviser is held to no such standard. When a financial adviser is a fiduciary, it means they are duty-bound always to put the client's interest first, and they must fully disclose all fees and potential conflicts of interest. Neither product company interests, nor their own company's interests would be placed ahead of your own.

All of this is not to say that brokers or sales people who are not fiduciaries are bad and fiduciaries alone are good. They're simply serving different purposes. When you go into an appliance store, you want a salesperson to advise you on the nuances of different products. But with the complexities of financial products and their huge impact on your life, you want to work with an adviser who is focused on knowing and protecting your well being, like a fiduciary, not like a salesperson who is focused on knowing and selling a product. Surveys have shown that the vast majority of financial consumers assume that their banks, their brokerage firms and financial advisers are acting in a fiduciary capacity when that is not true. They are acting like salespeople. The ruse has worked to the financial advantage of these large companies, but at the consumer's expense.

In short, the term "financial adviser" means very little. They are generally not fiduciaries for their clients and are rarely trained comprehensively or holistically as Certified Financial Planners® (CFP®) or Registered Life Planners® (RLP®). (Refer to the **Life Planning** and **Professional Designations** sections in this chapter for more detail.) These generic financial advisers are still tied to commissions, and their companies make money (in addition to advice fees) on trades or trading relationships, and that creates conflicts of interest with the advice the consumer needs and deserves. This generic adviser also has biases toward certain kinds of investments and investment products – particularly those sold by their company – which are often more expensive than alternative approaches would be. The allegiance of such "advisers" is to the financial company that employs them rather than to the customers they advise.

I'm sure that this makes it sound challenging to get a fair shake when buying financial products. That was true in the past. But it's not true anymore. The major tool an adviser has to assure you that you are being well served is full disclosure, which is a requirement for fiduciaries. A fiduciary discloses all potential conflicts of interest to the client. That is what any great adviser will do. For example, if the adviser has few conflicts, they might say: "I use only mutual funds that carry no commissions. I receive no money from any of the products I sell. My compensation comes entirely from the fee we work out between us. I work for you. You pay me directly. No one else pays me anything." This is the kind of disclosure you receive from a fee-only adviser. If, on the other hand, a financial adviser claims: "There are no fees," or "It doesn't cost anything to work with me," move on quickly. If they say they are a fiduciary, ask to see the disclosure documents that show exactly what you are paying, exactly what the adviser gets paid and whether there are any "mystery players" who get paid (or who pay the adviser) even though you don't know what they do.

Some History on Fees

In the 1970s, a small group of independent advisers began to charge "fees" for their services rather than "sales commissions" in an attempt to show consumers the difference: Salesmen sell products; independent fiduciaries sell advice.

This independent movement swelled in the 1980s, when more and more elite planners joined the fee-only advisers. These planners were fiduciaries for their clients: The client's interest always came first. So, the salesperson, too, began charging fees and advertising it. But they were just muddying the waters. What they failed to advertise was that their fees were on top of commissions and that they still didn't qualify as fiduciaries. See the *More on Fees* section later in this chapter for more detail.

So how do you find a fiduciary? Pretty easy. All RIAs (Registered Investment Advisers) are fiduciaries. Members of the National Association of Personal Financial Advisers (NAPFA) are also required to sign a fiduciary oath. (See below.) Most of the time Certified Financial Planners® are fiduciaries as well. Refer to *Professional Designations* section later in this chapter for more detail.

Who aren't fiduciaries? Insurance agents, stock brokers and registered representatives of broker dealers.

The Committee for the Fiduciary Standard (http://fiduciary.hb2web. net/) recommends getting in writing your adviser's commitment to the standard. If your adviser is not an RIA or a NAPFA member, they suggest you get them to sign off on the following fiduciary oath establishing their commitment to putting your interests first. And, finally, beware of advisers who wear two hats, who claim to be fiduciaries when they are "giving advice" but are not fiduciaries when they sell you a product.

PUTTING YOUR INTERESTS FIRST

◆◆◆◆◆

I believe in placing your best interests first. Therefore, I am proud to commit to the following five fiduciary principles:

I will always put your best interests first.

I will act with prudence; that is, with the skill, care, diligence, and good judgment of a professional.

I will not mislead you, and I will provide conspicuous, full and fair disclosure of all important facts.

I will avoid conflicts of interest.

I will fully disclose and fairly manage, in your favor, any unavoidable conflicts.

Advisor   ---------------------------

Firm Affiliation   ---------------------------

Date   ---------------------------

The Integrity Myth

The Integrity Myth goes like this: *It all comes down to personal integrity. If the adviser has it, regardless of the company he works for, you'll get good advice.* True enough, but a statement like this from an adviser generally is asking a consumer to take unnecessary risk in their choice of advisers. I was at a global conference on financial planning a few years ago where a financial planner from Australia speaking to other financial planners summed up my thoughts pretty well. He said, "Look, we all know that a fiduciary who is a fee-based, fee-transparent financial planner can do just as good a job as a fee-only planner will do. But when a client walks into our office and hears this: 'Not only do we not receive commissions of any kind, but we have no ties to product companies of any kind as well. We are paid only by you,' The client lets out a huge sigh of relief and says, 'Thank goodness.'" As an adviser, why wouldn't you want to give your clients that degree of assurance, and as a client, why would you want to settle for anything less?

Conflict of Interest Caveat

Although it should be obvious that a product and commission structure to compensation will carry the most conflicts of interest, it should be pointed out that no one is totally free of conflict. All advisers would prefer that you hire them rather than not hire them for their personal financial reasons at the very least. Advisers have other conflicts as well. Suppose one of their clients deposited $1 million with them; another client, $50,000. Will the broker/adviser give more attention to the larger client, the one who pays larger fees because the fees are based on a percentage of assets under management? Will the wealthier client get the first call-back with a problem? Even the decision by a client to pay off a mortgage presents conflicts. If a client takes $150,000 out of their investment account to pay back their mortgage, they have $150,000 less invested with the adviser and the adviser loses money on management fees if that is an element of or influence on their charging structure.

2. The "Why Should You Care about Fees, It's the Returns that Matter?" Fallacy

This is an argument used time and again to hoodwink consumers into paying higher fees than necessary for financial products. At first it sounds compelling. After all, of course, what we all want is the best return, and the higher fees are worth it. But a Morningstar.com report of August 9, 2010 put this argument to bed for good. Morningstar makes its money giving ratings to mutual funds, helping both consumers and advisers pick funds to invest in. What their August 2010 study shows is that low-cost funds beat high-cost funds, including Morningstar's own picks, in every time period. A related finding is that the amount you pay in fees to a mutual fund company is a better predictor of future fund performance than the mutual fund's track record. The higher the fees you pay, the lower your long-term return will be.

So as a consumer, what do you do? Look for quality, but go where the fees are lowest as well. Better yet find an adviser whose fees are low and whose passion is to find the lowest cost, highest quality products for your portfolio. That's one of the advantages of a fee-only adviser. You pay them a fee for their advice. It's then their primary incentive to save you money as they earn you money. They will automatically look for the least expensive products that are likely to produce the best results for you. Refer to **More on Fees** section later in this chapter for more detail.

Conflict of Interest

When looking for a good financial adviser, the first thing the consumer should do is determine where that adviser has conflicts of interest. The most obvious conflict for a financial planner is if they are rewarded more richly for selling one product than another. This was a common problem in the past when the wirehouses (an archaic term for broker dealers who used the telegraph wires to make trades) sold "house products" such as mutual funds and insurance annuities that were labeled "Merrill Lynch Growth Fund," for instance. Typically, a wirehouse offered both its own house products and products from other vendors. But the "house" wanted clients to buy the house funds. So it paid higher commissions for these funds to its advisers. That way, the brokerage made more money because it also collected management fees for its funds. To make them more attractive to brokers, the brokerage padded the house products with special fees and commissions that similar products from other vendors didn't carry. So the client of this broker got a double dose of conflicts. The brokerage made more money and the broker made more money with these "house funds." Who do you think paid that extra money?

Partly because of the higher fees and also because the house managers are usually not as talented as outside mutual fund managers, most house products do not perform well. And, in addition, financial product salespeople are awarded fancy vacations and other bonuses for putting customer money in a house product. This structure works very well for the wirehouse and the broker. Both get bigger fees and commissions. Only the client suffers: He gets an investment dud at a high price.

In March of 2012 The National Bureau of Economic Research released a study of financial advisers, exploring their biases and conflicts of interest. Their conclusions should be sobering to anyone looking for an adviser:

"financial advisers exploit the biases of naïve (or uninformed) retail investors"

"our evidence suggests that adviser self-interest plays an important role in generating advice that is not in the best interest of the clients"

And from the Abstract summary of their study:

"Advisers encourage returns-chasing behavior and push for actively managed funds that have higher fees, even if the client starts with a well-diversified low-fee portfolio."

Commission Advisers

An "adviser" who gets paid by commissions receives a fee as a consequence of the sale of a financial product. Thus he is more appropriately described as a salesperson than an adviser. We've already spoken at some length about the conflicts of interest such forms of charging bring to advice. Here are two resources you might explore that give great clarity as to how commission conflicts can dramatically influence an adviser's recommendations to you.

The first is a webinar by Greenspring Wealth, a fee-only advisory firm in Maryland: http://greenspringwealth.com/greenspring-u/webinar/the -conflicted-world-of-financial-services/. In it you will see examples from Merrill Lynch, Edward Jones and Wells Fargo, but similar examples could be drawn from many brokers. It is easy to see, and shocking to consider, how a shift in product choice can hugely impact adviser compensation in ways that threaten your own interests as a consumer. It is a healthy reminder that the last thing you want for your adviser is a compensation structure that favors one product over another.

The second resource is the work of Joshua Brown, one of the leaders in the movement of brokers away from the large institutions with their product orientation and their sales incentives to the fee-only world of client service and investment advice. To understand how the commission driven world views consumers, buy his book: Backstage Wall Street (2012). And go to his blog: www.thereformedbroker.com. You will become a fee-only convert, if you were not convinced already.

There are two very positive things to say about commissions. The first is that even there you will on occasion find terrific planners, RLPs®, CFPs® and fiduciaries, with complete transparency in their fee structure and who work with middle-income clients. One such person is Mary Zimmerman in Arizona. I've known and worked with Mary for years, have consulted her as I wrote this book, and have not hesitated to recommend clients to her. The other thing to say about commissions is if you know exactly, or very closely, what it is you want in a financial product and don't need advice, a commissioned salesperson may be the least expensive of your choices, other than doing it yourself with a no-load, no commission product. But you may need an adviser rather than a salesperson to tell you whether a commissioned salesperson is indeed the cheapest way to purchase a financial product!

3. *The Large Institution Fallacy*

"Those on the front line dealing with clients believe they are doing, and want to do, the right thing. It's the institution that is getting between the client and the broker."

Harold Evensky

You will occasionally find a terrific adviser at a large institution, including CFPs® and RLPs®, *but the odds are stacked against you here as well.*

Consumers gravitate toward the large institutions under the false impression that these institutions are both more secure and more professional than independent advisers. (Just like my innocent belief as a child that Merrill Lynch could take care of everything for me if I were orphaned.) This false impression has somewhat miraculously survived the banking crisis. Never mind the institutions that have collapsed, failed to maintain a fiduciary relationship with customers and even demanded money from taxpayers to set them afloat. These institutional "advisers" won't mention to you that you would need to hire an independent specialist to analyze the weaknesses of their institution's "structured" products because the products have been engineered to hide these weaknesses or costs often even from the "advisers" who sell them. As for your "great returns," there's not a large firm out there (with the exception of a rare and idiosyncratic mutual fund or hedge fund that you could never have picked in advance) that has the numbers to prove that they as a firm have delivered a return better than the average return of the market as a whole over the past 20 years.

The truth is that your assets, managed by an independent CFP® and an RLP®, are just as protected at a discount brokerage firm such as Scottrade, Charles Schwab, TD Ameritrade, Zecco or Sharebuilder as they are at a full-service brokerage institution. And you have the added advantage of working with a genuine adviser, not a sales person.

Investing with large institutions puts all your financial decisions at higher risk because you are not getting objective, *fiduciary* advice on the products or services you acquire. Further, large institutions rarely have the full set of no-load (no commission) or low-cost products you can find elsewhere or through an independent adviser.

The primary interest of these large institutions is to make money. For example, for 70 years the full-service brokerages fought against accepting a fiduciary obligation to their clients. In July 2004, the Financial Planning Association (FPA) sued the SEC for allowing brokers who collected fees for their accounts in addition to commissions to ignore the fiduciary standard. In 2007, the court ruled for the FPA and against the SEC. But that didn't stop the SEC from allowing brokers to continue to operate with two hats (one being a commissioned broker, the other a "fiduciary" appearance while avoiding the regulation requirements for a fiduciary.)

During the 2008 banking crisis companies were exposed for selling mortgages that were destined to collapse due to lack of underwriting standards, and then those same companies foreclosed on homes when people couldn't afford to pay. Any individual who claimed to be giving you fiduciary advice on a product sold by their own company and then tried to take away your property would probably find themselves in jail for fraud. But if their name was Bank of America, Citigroup, Fannie Mae, Freddie Mac or a host of others, settlements were made and the fraud was often overlooked. This "pretending to give advice but really selling product game" has been going on for decades. What wishful thinking makes anyone suspect it's stopped now?

4. The Active Investing Fallacy (or the Advantages of Passive Investing)

People often ask advisers which mutual fund will make them winners, which is the best to buy now. The truth is that no one can predict the direction of the stock market or the performance of a particular stock or mutual fund. A successful investor needs a collection of investments that make up a diversified portfolio. They should resist frequent trading in their portfolio, which drives up costs, and purchasing the "hot funds" touted by magazines and television programs that have run their course and are headed for a rest. There are no guarantees that a fund will perform in the future as it has in the past. A fund that has recently exploded on the upside might lose 10% the day after you buy it. We don't know what will happen to the stock market. An interesting example is the Fidelity Magellan fund, which turned in such a stellar record in the 1980s that it became a household name – and the fund to buy now. It ran into trouble when the fund became too large to manage efficiently. In 2008, the fund lost 49.66%. It is no longer the hot fund.

Many consumers reasoned that if they couldn't pick the top funds themselves they needed to hire someone to help. They could see only one reason to engage a financial planner: To get better investment results. But the truth is finding a great adviser is not about "beating the market." Rather it is about the whole variety of financial services that determine how the adviser will help you find and deliver the life and lifestyle that you want by integrating your financial decisions with your personal ones. Among those services is an investment program and a client/adviser relationship that gives you the confidence to hold on to your investments in rough and volatile markets.

Consider what happened in 2008. The Standard & Poor's 500-stock index lost 38.91% for the year. Worse yet, it kept sinking in 2009 until March when the S&P 500 hit 666 on a truly grim day. Many investors, in total despair, bailed out. Then the market reversed direction and began to climb again. Few of us felt confident in our investments during that dismal period. Those who bailed out on or even near that fateful day lost the most money. By the time they were ready to dive back in, the market had recovered losses and that investor would never catch up. One important job of a financial adviser is to create a compelling investment proposition and a terrific relationship with you that give you the confidence to hang on in the most challenging times because we never know when the market will change direction. Let's consider some of the ingredients you might find in such a compelling proposition.

There are many important factors to consider when choosing investments. Among the most important is how much they cost. The lowest-cost funds deliver the highest returns in their categories over the long run. They are typically index funds, which are funds that invest passively in an entire sector of the market. One index could invest in large company stocks in the US, another exclusively in bonds, another in emerging markets or in a single country such as Brazil or Russia. By investing passively, the fund manager sets up the fund based on the index or market sector and then resists tinkering with it. The opposite strategy, active investing, means that the fund manager trades the securities in the fund actively to attempt to beat the market. Actively managed funds cost more because a portfolio manager must be paid for picking the securities, and the more frequent trading adds to the cost. Active funds will cost you more in taxes as well. Unless held in retirement accounts, each trade for profit is a taxable event.

Low-cost index funds are offered by many fund companies. They are low-cost because there is little trading. An index fund is set up to follow an index such as the Standard & Poor's Index of 500 stocks and it moves along with that index, never outperforming the index. (It underperforms the index slightly due to the management fees.)

If you were to invest in a simple passive portfolio yourself you might choose three low cost index funds: a US equity fund, an international equity fund and a bond fund. Buy and hold them. This would be a low cost, purely passive route. The danger is that it would likely carry greater temptations for you to sell at market bottoms and buy at market tops than working with the steady focus and dedication of an adviser who might invest you in a dozen or more funds, balanced for the long run in such a way to require virtually no trading at all.

Of course there is a downside to this consistent, diversified approach. The return is what critics might call mediocre, at least in any particular year. An important concept in investing is that risk and return play against each other. An actively managed fund with a high-powered fund manager might be able to shoot the lights out over a short time period. But the downside can be just as dramatic. On average only 35% of fund managers beat the market in any given year. And they are rarely the same ones year after year. In fact, over a longer time frame Citywire reported that 93% of active global equity funds failed to beat the MSCI World Index over a ten year period from October 2001 to October 2011. Many investors adhere to a strategy that attempts to catch the high-flying stocks. They might use "momentum" investing, or jumping on board as a stock is headed up. Perhaps they favor "technical" investing, or picking stocks based on quantitative factors that they measure with charts and graphs. These are all legitimate ways to invest. But they require a great deal of research and investment knowledge and they are anything but foolproof. Indeed, it is an extremely rare fund manager who can deliver explosive growth (or even beat the market) year after year.

The cost of owning a fund is called the expense ratio. This is money that comes out of the fund every year – whether the fund goes up or down – to pay expenses. Index funds generally have very low expense ratios, sometimes as low as (or lower than) 20 basis points, whereas actively managed equity (stock) mutual funds average 150 to 200 basis points. (A basis point is 1/100th of 1% so 20 basis points amounts to 20/100 of 1 percent or an annual fee of $2.00 on your $1000 investment, whereas 200 basis points would amount to 2% or a $20 fee on your investment.) The difference may seem like small potatoes but it can make the difference between a good return over many years and a mediocre or poor return over the same time period.

This is why low expenses are one hallmark of investment success. Passive management, which usually goes hand in hand with low expenses, is another one. Vanguard was the first retail fund company to use passive investing, or index funds, under founder and former chairman John C. Bogle. Bogle introduced the first index fund for retail investors in 1976. That fund, Vanguard Index 500, duplicates the performance of the Standard & Poor's 500 Index because it holds the same stocks as the index, just slightly underperforming due to the fund's management expenses. Investors were slow to embrace index funds. But by the end of 2010, Vanguard 500 had $102.6 billion in assets.

Institutional investors, such as pension funds, pour billions of dollars into low-cost index funds like those offered by Dimensional Fund Advisers (DFA). Retail investors cannot buy directly from DFA. The fund company restricts access to institutions and fee-only financial advisers whom the company has researched and deemed worthy of offering their funds. DFA believes that dealing through professional investors will reduce frequent trading in the funds and manage cash flows better. These measures lower trading costs and also improve tax efficiency – the more uncontrolled trades in a fund the more likely you will be paying capital gains on them.

Vanguard and other fund companies began offering myriad other indexes such as one that follows the total domestic market as well as a new instrument, called an electronically traded fund (ETF), that allows investors to put money in large and small markets all over the world. Mutual funds are priced at the end of every trading day and cannot be traded during regular market hours. They are traded directly with the fund company. In contrast, ETFs are priced throughout the trading day and trade on national exchanges so that you can buy them like a stock.

Rick Ferri, founder of the investment firm Portfolio Solutions and a Forbes columnist, published a book in 2011 called *The Power of Passive Investing: More Wealth with Less Work* (2010). Although Ferri acknowledges that the fear of being nothing more than average haunts index funds, he provides a powerful list of reasons why investors who want good, steady returns over time should embrace indexing by looking at the performance of the Vanguard 500 for the 25 years ending in 2009.

Ferri notes these problems with active funds:

Performance: Measured by raw returns – not considering taxes or risk – the index funds out performed two-thirds of the active funds. One-third of the funds overperformed. But funds cannot be measured based purely on their raw returns. The funds must also be tested for taxes and risk. If one fund took on significantly higher risk to achieve a higher return, the returns are not comparable. Risk is one of the most counter-intuitive aspects of performance returns. A first impulse might be to say: "I'll take the top fund. Forget the risk." Because performance matters more, right?

But a higher risk investment has the same potential for higher losses on the negative side as for higher gains on the positive side, due to the risk, which goes both ways.

Taxes are also a consideration. Because actively traded funds trade more – about 50% turnover a year for active funds vs. 6% for index funds – the active funds cost more on an after-tax basis. Moreover, funds distribute these taxable gains to shareholders. The after-tax cost per year over a 15-year period was 1.5% for active funds and 0.5% for index funds, according to the Morningstar Tax Cost Ratio. If these costs are included, Ferri estimates that the Vanguard 500 beat over 90% of active funds over the 25 years ending in 2009. Of course, even though a small percentage of funds do beat the 500 index each year, they are not the same ones. If we could name 10 funds – or even 5 funds – that beat the S&P index every year over the last 10 years, that would be pretty exciting. But performance of actively managed funds varies from year to year as the market environment changes, a new manager arrives, or sometimes when the fund becomes too large. Several studies have shown that fund size is a predictor of performance, with smaller funds typically doing better thanks to their agility in trading. Large funds – especially really large funds – typically lag.

Costs: Ferri reports that John Bogle calculated the returns of actively managed funds vs. the S&P 500 Index over the 30 years ending in 1975. The funds underperformed the index on an annual pre-tax margin by 1.5%, a number identical with the costs charged by active funds. In addition, active funds often include sales or commission charges, added to the price of the fund, as well as exit fees in some cases. And, if not held in a tax-deferred account, you may have taxes to pay each year on their active trading.

Years ago, critics said that there were too few index funds to create a diversified portfolio. They may have been right. But in 2011, there were well over 1,000 index funds and exchange-traded funds (ETFs) available from dozens of different companies. Allan Roth, author of *How a Second Grader Beats Wall Street: Golden Rules Any Investor Can Learn* (2011), calculated the probability that a randomly selected portfolio of actively managed funds would beat an all index fund portfolio. His results? A portfolio of five active funds has a 32% chance of beating the index fund in one year; by ten years, the chance for the five-fund portfolio to win is 11%. Roth shows that the more funds you hold and the longer the time period, the less chance you have of beating a market index. So it is that a portfolio of ten active funds has a 1% chance of beating an indexed portfolio over 25 years.

Finally, as we've mentioned, the 2010 study by Morningstar found that low fees are the most dependable indicator of a mutual fund's performance. Morningstar studied fees and performance during various time periods from 2005 through March 2010. Over every period and in every asset class — domestic equity, international equity, balanced, taxable bond and municipal bond — the cheapest funds, as a group, produced higher total returns than the most expensive group.

Bottom Line

In the old days, brokers would "pick stocks" for a client earning a nice commission on each trade. The worst of them churned their accounts with rapid trades, earning massive commissions, an unethical practice sometimes known as "churning, earning and burning." Nowadays most advisers simply employ an "asset allocation" strategy that buys and holds mutual funds for longer time periods, although there can be just as costly rapid trading within the mutual funds themselves. Keep in mind, neither past performance nor future strategies are good predictors of future returns.

When it comes to investing you will want to consider carefully the passive route of index funds and ETFs, and weigh just as carefully the investment philosophy of your potential financial adviser against the benchmark of indexing. You will find as many differences within the camps of active and passive investing, as you will between them. One thing is clear, however, as you move from sales to service and advice, the closer you come to a pure advice model, the less trading activity you will find in the portfolio.

You will find that a high percentage of planners who are Registered Life Planners® have a passive orientation in their investing, as do members of the Garrett Planning Network, the Cambridge Connection, the IFP (Institute of Financial Planning) and NAPFA. Refer to the *Life Planning* section later in this chapter for more detail.

5. *The Best Friend Fallacy*

Sometimes people choose a financial adviser based on personal recommendation or personal connection, and as a result do not pay attention to the qualifications of the adviser or the nature of the company in which they work. They believe the personal connection guarantees great service. This is perhaps the hardest of all fallacies to counter. In fact I seldom try anymore. For me it unfortunately often comes down to having a disagreement with a dear friend that risks losing that friendship (or altering it for years), while fighting for something you'll never win anyway because of the attachment that has formed between the client and their adviser. Given my low odds of changing things, I'd rather mention my difference of opinion lightly, but aim to keep the friendship and see how else I can be of service. But this is the question you should ask yourself: *"Would you rather have a friend who is merely associated with a hospital handle an illness you've discovered in yourself, or would you seek out a doctor or specialist who is fully qualified to treat the disease?"*

Another way of thinking about this is as if each financial services company is a huge hospital without a doctor in it, but filled with likeable people who will sell you equipment, drugs or surgery. Who would be fool enough to buy? And yet routinely consumers let large financial institutions do just that, sell them products rather than understand, diagnose, analyze and then deliver the freedom into their clients' lives that the clients most desire.

Just in the past 10 years I've had three dear friends who have fallen prey to the "best friend fallacy." Each in turn has called me eventually, saying "Please help me, I should have taken your advice." One of them had a benefactor recommend a financial adviser, for another it was their dear uncle's adviser, for another the adviser was her brother. None of the advisers was a Life Planner, a Certified Financial Planner®, or a fiduciary. All of them worked for large firms that sold products. Two of them encouraged their clients to take out loans, either mortgages or margin loans to keep their portfolio's size (and the adviser's fees) large. One of them encouraged their client to buy and sell products rapidly, bringing lots of commission money to the adviser and to his firm. Each friend lost more than half their money before calling me again for my advice.

When the stock market crashed in October of 2008, a friend of Mary Rowland, Wendy, told her she was happy to have all her money invested in a safe place where it wasn't affected by market turmoil. Before her father died, he told Wendy that he had invested her inheritance with a good friend and trusted adviser and she needn't worry about it. "I don't know how Bernard Madoff keeps producing these returns," she said. "He's magic." Madoff was not only "a friend." He also had extraordinary credentials in the financial product world as former Chairman of both the National Association of Securities Dealers (NASD), and the NASDAQ stock exchange.

In December of 2008 it was revealed that Madoff allegedly lost $52 billion of client money in a Ponzi scheme. "I'm a crook," Madoff told FBI agents. Madoff claimed he worked alone to bilk investors, charities, banks, and other entities around the world. But it later became clear that he had help. A lot of people kept mum about this gigantic fraud.

Wendy had lived a comfortable but not ostentatious life with the proceeds of her trust fund but lost both her regular quarterly income as well as her $5 million inheritance. She had about $6,000 remaining in her checking account and no work experience. But now at least she knows how Madoff produced the magic: He recruited new investor money to send to earlier investors, pretending that it was a return on their investment. To make his scheme work, he needed a constant flow of fresh money to send to previous investors, claiming it was "income." Securities examiners said there is no evidence that Madoff invested or traded any of the $50 billion plus that he claims he collected with his scheme.

When the market began to sink at the end of 2007, Madoff's investors began to ask for their money back. By the fall of 2008, when banks, insurance companies, investment banks, auto companies and you-name-it began to fail and the world economy teetered on the brink of collapse, too many Madoff investors asked for a return of their principal at the same time. Madoff frantically tried to raise new money to return principal and pay returns to the investors who stayed, taking new deposits as recently as nine days before his firm tanked. But he couldn't keep up with the cash outflow.

Most financial advisers are good people. The Madoffs are the exceptions. More often than not, advisers are well meaning and have a good deal of training in personal finance that fits the products their company is most interested in promoting, the products that provide the highest incentives for selling. James Norton, based in London, a partner at EVOLVE, one of the great young firms in the UK, with multiple RLPs® and CFPs® in the firm, was a transaction (commission) driven adviser for six years before he changed his approach. He said to me, "George, I'm the same person now that I was then." I know James. He is professional, caring, thoughtful, kind, concerned. He was that way when he worked with commissions just as much as afterward. It was not that James became a better person, but that he woke up to the realization that there was a better way to respond to his clients' needs. Bernie Madoff turned out not to be a great friend to choose as a financial adviser. The problem is that if you have not looked at your friends as carefully as you would any other financial adviser you were considering, using the criteria I listed above, you will not know you have made a poor choice until it is too late.

There is a version of the "Best Friend Fallacy" that is used by nearly everyone these days, because of the low level of repute that financial services have fallen into. It goes like this. "My adviser's OK, I like her (or him), but I don't trust the rest of them or the industry as a whole."

Most financial advisers are well liked. So are most salespeople. Their livelihood depends on it. Is our general mistrust misguided? Or is liking our adviser not an adequate evaluation of their professional qualities, and, in particular, of those qualities that would deliver us the financial architecture and the freedom we need in our lives to live at our greatest potential. The problem is that most of us don't know what those essential qualities or qualifications are, nor how to judge an adviser's likelihood of having them! And so we trust our own adviser until he disappoints us in some way or economic circumstances turn against us in a way that he hadn't prepared us for, our dream of freedom unrealized. Typically, a client likes their adviser until the bottom falls out and then leaves the adviser at a crucial or unfortunate moment. In the rarest and most unfortunate of circumstances, the client suddenly realizes – as those of Bernie Madoff did – that the adviser has dramatically failed them, or even stolen their money. Often this change happens at a market bottom, where we sell out, only to buy back in with another "adviser" when the market, months or years later, is at a peak: A losing strategy if there ever was one, but a common one.

So my question to you is this: Is "But they're my friend!" a responsible answer to who will manage your financial resources into old age, protect your children and heirs, and provide you the maximum benefit over your life now and in retirement? Is that a good argument to weigh against the fact that they aren't an RLP®, a CFP®, a fiduciary, fee-only, and that they don't use the lowest cost products, but instead use in-company products, "sophisticated," "clever" products that even they do not understand? You owe it to yourself, your own dream of freedom and to your family to abandon the "Best Friend Fallacy" right now, and find a proper adviser to deliver and secure your future.

6. *The Do-It-Yourself and the News/Advice Fallacy*

Although much of *Life Planning for You* has a self-help flavor, I believe strongly that most of us need a financial adviser. I myself have employed one since I sold my advisory firm fourteen years ago. It's not that I couldn't do much of the work myself, and do it well, but

1. It's not the best use of my time. Writing books, training advisers to do Life Planning, spending time with my children, all have greater value for me.

2. Even with all my knowledge and years of experience, without constant attention I will miss new tax rules, insurance and investment opportunities because I won't be able to keep up.

3. My adviser provides reporting for taxes and spreadsheets for economic decisions for me that I don't have to do myself and that I can access almost at the drop of a hat.

4. I can call my adviser at any time, and make quick and clear decisions as necessary, or explore more complex areas over time.

5. My anxiety level is dramatically reduced knowing I have a firm, a system and a person I can trust.

A few other reasons to consider:

1. If you do your investing yourself, you will be tempted to get out of markets when they look terrible and your future looks bleak and you feel you can't afford even one more dollar of loss (just the time to get into the market). And you will get into markets just when they look most promising, most alluring, when they have delivered solid value for so long you bet it will never stop, but in fact that is just when they are peaking.

2. If you are out of the market at its bottom you might be proud of yourself but it is often the first 10 days of a bull market explosion that delivers the great returns you receive from stocks. Miss those 10 days, and you miss a lot.

3. Without a Life Planner's support most people don't claim their "last 5% of freedom," what makes them feel truly fulfilled, accomplished and alive. This is the most important criterion of all. Do you have a financial architecture that delivers you into the freedom that you are most passionate to experience, with all of your vitality and your genius propelled into the world?

4. If you rely on the media for financial recommendations, you are generally relying on someone who is not a CFP®, nor a professional investor, not an RLP®, nor a fiduciary.

5. If you rely on the media, often you will be getting advice that is limited in time (just the day it's being given), without obligation or knowledge as to when the recommendation might change.

6. If you rely on the media, you will never be getting comprehensive financial advice based upon your own and your family's specific and personal situation.

7. Reporters are pushed by editors to come up with the "next new thing" in investments even if it doesn't necessarily serve readers well. Magazine cover stories trumpeting "the fund to buy now" are worthless. They are designed to sell magazines or sell advertising and boost newsstand sales. When magazines conduct focus groups to find out which potential cover story lines draw the most readers, two areas get maximum response: What to do with your money and how to diet/exercise/improve health. Cover lines that promise vast riches and perfect health should be abolished!

For most of us, the ideal would be to find a financial adviser, a system and a firm we can trust, modest in cost, to whom we can efficiently outsource all of our concerns regarding personal finance, someone who cares about our purposes in life and encourages us in effective ways to pursue them wholly and completely. One of the reasons that we choose advisers poorly, or that we choose to do our financial work ourselves, can be that we've failed to think deeply or clearly about money, its place in our lives and what we want from it. We project that lack of clarity onto our advisers (including a confused mix of parental projections, hope for our future, distrust of all financial people and awe of their financial "skills" or mystifications), so we don't really know what we want from them, or what we require of them. As a result, we're satisfied by someone who's a pretty nice person, with a professional manner and plenty of graphs and charts, who remembers the name of our spouse and kids and gives the impression of being on top of things most of the time. Perhaps we're satisfied merely with the size of the firm, or the quality of the view or the furniture.

These are terrible reasons to pick an adviser. These mistaken views come from thinking that money is about spreadsheets and total return and the latest products that promise to protect us no matter whether the market goes up or down; that the best money decisions come from experts in leather chairs with great views. Almost as if we are in a dream, what we have forgotten is that money is about our lives.

Money is about us. It's meant to be the great facilitator between the world and us – the facilitator of our becoming and being who we want to be, doing the things that we love, bringing all our vitality, all of our passion and our heart into being. We've been looking in the wrong place for help around money, because we're mystified by its aura, rather than being clear and direct about who we are, who we want to be, what we want from our money and what we want from our advisers. For money to work well for us, we need the quality of a mentor as well as all the other financial skills we seek in an adviser. We need someone who will make sure we use our money to become who we are meant to be. We need advisers who are wise in life as well as wise in the way of money.

Life Planning

In May of 2013 the Association of Financial Advisers (AFA) in Australia issued a white paper called The Trusted Adviser. It explored a very simple question in a survey of 512 clients of 13 of the very best advisers in Australia, as measured by their ranking in the Adviser of the Year awards from 2012 and 2011. The question: "What are the qualities of your adviser that are most important to you?" With an 82% response rate, overwhelming all other categories (including knowledge, reputation, service, technical expertise and experience) was "interpersonal skills" which included "communication skills, building rapport, caring about clients, understanding needs, listening, empathy."

The good news for people looking for a financial adviser who will have great interpersonal skills is that there now exist designations for planners who have been trained to listen and to look at your entire life, to help you see how you can use financial savvy to go after your dreams rather than just socking money away for a comfy retirement. At the risk of being self serving, the Kinder Institute of Life Planning has created and developed one of them – the RLP® or Registered Life Planner® designation.

What Makes an RLP® Different?

The EVOKE® process that you've experienced in this book is the Kinder Institute's method of teaching RLPs® how to do Life Planning. As advisers they are trained in the human skills of listening, empathy and inspiration, as well as the dedication to deliver their clients into "freedom." They each have experienced first-hand as part of their training the power and exhilaration that comes from being Life Planned. They themselves have felt a Life Planner support and inspire and help launch them into the life they've always wanted to live. If you have felt some of that thrill as you have done the exercises in this book, then you can understand the value of working with an adviser who places your life ahead of your money

One of the wonderful things about EVOKE® is that it is a systematic, replicable model, a process that everyone in a firm can use, not just your individual adviser. If anything were to happen to your adviser, you would want to know that others in the firm are trained in EVOKE® or that your adviser had a succession plan with someone who was also a Life Planner, and held the same values and designations that brought you to your adviser.

Most often the RLP® will be a Certified Financial Planner® (and/or Chartered in the UK) and will do the financial work as well. Occasionally they will outsource pieces of the work to another member of their firm or to a specialist. The RLP® designation doesn't come with its own financial system, but once you've identified your goals and envisioned your Life Plan, you will go through all the financial planning steps to get there, including cash flow analysis, budgeting, risk management, estate planning, taxes, investing and other financial questions for specific purposes such as college tuition and retirement needs.

Advisers in the RLP® program go through a two day workshop deepening listening skills and goal work, a five day EVOKE® training (limited to a dozen participants) where each adviser practices the process of Life Planning another while getting Life Planned themselves, and then a six month mentorship embedding the process in their business using real life case studies. We have found it to be as critical for client service for a Life Planner to be Life Planned and live their Life Plan, as it is for them to embed the Life Planning ethos in their business.

Where to Find an RLP®

If you want an RLP®, someone fully trained in the EVOKE® process, start with the list of over 300 RLPs® on www.KinderInstitute.com. RLPs® have spent a good deal of resources and energy to gain this designation, and to do truly client-centered work. So these folks are motivated to help change peoples' lives. The majority of RLPs® are also trained financial advisers.

Suppose there is no RLP® in your area. The Kinder Institute has trained over 2000 planners across 25 countries and six continents in at least two days worth of Life Planning training, with special emphasis on listening and goal-setting skills. Most of these, too, are listed on www.KinderInstitute.com. You are likely to find someone nearby from this list. If you don't, many Kinder trained advisers use Skype to work over long distances with clients. Choosing someone at a distance, particularly if they excel in all of the qualities of trust and practice that you seek, is preferable to someone less qualified closer to home.

Other Resources

If you still come up empty handed, look at other planners and coaches who take a similar approach by putting your life ahead of your money. Many financial advisers have come to realize that money issues are more about change and emotions than about dollars and cents. Each may pursue their own method of Life Planning. Here are some of those who have designed programs for financial advisers to strengthen their Life Planning skills:

Susan Bradley, a Certified Financial Planner® with two decades of experience, realized that she did not have the right training to help clients cope with major life events that involved money. Sure she knew how to plan for retirement and invest and buy insurance and all the other money issues that clients face. Her website SuddenMoney.com includes a list of planners – as well as wealth coaches and psychologists and attorneys – who have been through her program. Not surprisingly some of the same names appear on several different training programs. For example, Beth Jones, owner of Third Eye Associates in New York, has been trained by Bradley. She is also a CFP® and an RLP®, as is Lisa Kirchenbauer, owner of Omega Wealth Management in Virginia.

Dr. Ted Klontz is a financial psychologist who believes that we all have "money scripts," developed in childhood and that they prevent us from living the life we want to live. Dr. Klontz has developed tools to help us transform and rewire our money mindsets. He trains financial therapists and financial planners to use his system. He also provides many tips and ways to get started on his web site. His methods help clients evaluate their money disorders.

Rick Kahler became the first fee-only Certified Financial Planner® (CFP®) in South Dakota in 1983 when he set up the Kahler Financial Group. Kahler believes that financial therapy can help clients reduce anxiety about money and change financial behaviors. The author of four books, he offers weeklong seminars in "Healing Money Issues." Kahler believes that clients do best when they work with both a financial planner and a financial therapist. His web site at www.consciousfinance. com provides a list of financial planners and financial therapists that he recommends.

Carol Anderson developed the Money Quotient system in January 2001 to provide financial advisers and other professionals with tools and training to assist clients in developing a more successful and satisfying relationship with money. "Putting money in the context of life," is the tag phrase of the organization, which is a non-profit group charged with training professionals to work more successfully with clients. Many financial advisers such as Joan Sharp in Delaware, have been trained by Money Quotient as well as by the Kinder Institute. Marjorie Burnett, a financial Life Planner in Virginia, uses tools from both the Kinder Institute and Money Quotient, some for one thing, some for another. Burnett, a CFP® and RLP®, is also a CPA and an attorney.

Other trainers of financial advisers, generally considered part of the Life Planning revolution, include Mitch Anthony, Hugh Massie of Financial DNA, Roy Diliberto, Bill Bachrach and Maria Nemeth.

In addition to all these, the two largest professional associations of financial planners in America list many advisers trained in Life Planning skills.

NAPFA: The National Association of Personal Financial Advisers. NAPFA is the largest and the best known fee-only association in America with over 2400 members sworn to work on a fee-only basis. That means the advisers get no commissions, have minimal conflicts of interest and a fiduciary calling. In addition NAPFA members can take as many as 33 hours of Life Planning skills in their continuing education requirement of 60 hours every two years.

FPA: The Financial Planning Association. Like NAPFA, the FPA often has dedicated Life Planning tracks at its huge annual conference of Financial Planners. With 23,000 members you are likely to find an FPA adviser in your neighborhood.

More on Fees: How Financial Advisers Are Compensated and What It Means For You

Fee-Based Advisers

A fee-based adviser will charge you fees, but also charge you commissions on products. They can be just as riddled with conflicts of interest in giving you advice as a pure commissioned adviser, or they can be fee-transparent, which is a good thing. Some advisers use commission on products such as insurance to offset the fee. Few insurance products are sold without a commission.

Fee-Transparent Advisers

A fee-transparent adviser is one who reveals all conflicts of interest in detail to their customers; all fees and commissions are transparent and discussed openly as part of the decision-making process. The three major financial planning organizations in the US, NAPFA, the FPA and the Certified Financial Planner® Board of Standards have in the past disagreed about the proper way to charge for financial planning. But they have come together in the last few years regardless of their differences, all arguing for a fiduciary standard and for fee-transparency as the minimum requirement for a fiduciary to have in regard to charging clients for their services.

Fee-Only Advisers

A fee-only adviser does not take a commission for the sale of a financial product. They receive fees directly from the consumer for advisory services rendered. The three most common forms of fee-only structures are hourly, retainer, or a percentage charge for the total amount of assets under management (AUM) if the adviser is working as an investment adviser. If they invest your assets, they don't take custody of them. Custody is held by a discount broker in your own personal account. The adviser will have a limited trading authority for you, if you wish. They should seek out the least expensive products, with only the smallest commissions that go to the discount broker, not to the adviser. That's how the broker gets paid. The adviser gets paid only by you.

Good News on Fees for Middle-Market Consumers as Well

Many planners who committed to using fees rather than commissions met in Atlanta, GA in 1983 and formed the National Association of Personal Financial Advisers (NAPFA). Today this group, with about 2400 members, continues to work to elevate the reputation of financial advisers, partly by requiring that members charge only fees – no commissions allowed. NAPFA gained the respect of the media almost immediately. But of course there are many virtuous, fee-only planners who are not members of NAPFA. And there have been NAPFA members who fudged on the rules and worse! More about them in a moment.

If there were a kind of one-stop-shop, NAPFA with its fiduciary oath, its fee-only dedication and its "communication or counseling" Life Planning CEU requirement might be high on your list. Nearly all of its members are CFPs® as well.

One serious caveat regarding NAPFA, and a warning shot in your search for advisers from any association. Two former presidents of NAPFA have been charged with misdeeds including fraud. Both ran into trouble with risky illiquid investments.

Here are links to read more:

* http://www.nytimes.com/2011/10/22/your-money/financial-adviser-mark-spangler-accused-of-securities-fraud.html?pagewanted=all

* http://www.sec.gov/news/press/2012/2012-95.htm.

Evan Simonoff, editor of Financial Adviser magazine, wrote "It's unfair to tar a 2,000 member organization for the alleged behavior of two former presidents, but there are lessons here for all advisers," and for consumers we would add.

If you want the gold standard of fee-only advisers, search the NAPFA website, but exercise caution if in addition to publicly traded stocks, bonds and mutual funds, they also offer illiquid investments that you can't easily redeem or trade such as limited partnerships, hedge funds, proprietary products and private equity ventures. It is not that these are necessarily bad investments, but they carry more risk and require more caution and due diligence than many consumers can muster. If you want to keep your search simple, steer clear of advisers who offer these products. In addition often these investments a) cost more in advisory fees b) have had inadequate research to establish their value (certainly much less information is available on them than on publicly traded stocks or mutual funds) c) would require additional due diligence on your part so that you could feel confident that your adviser would be better than others who might dedicate their whole businesses to these kinds of investments, a truly unlikely prospect d) frequently contain layers of fees that may be hidden from your view e) may be neither liquid nor marketable f) have to be sold at a significant loss and subject you to unforeseen tax consequences if you change advisers as your new adviser is unlikely to know what to do with the investment.

That said, the fee-only movement pioneered by NAPFA has been one of the most genuinely consumer-oriented movements in financial services over the past 30 years, and has many great planners in it. Others followed in the steps of NAPFA. Better yet, some of them formed networks and trained others in their methods. Bert Whitehead did both. Whitehead, a lawyer with an MBA, has been practicing as a fee-only adviser in Michigan since 1972.

In 1995, he set up the Cambridge Connection, a group of fee-only advisers around the country whose aim is to bring holistic planning to middle-market Americans. When he started Cambridge Connection, Whitehead saw his mission as rescuing commission-based salespeople from "the dark side," by teaching them to survive and prosper on fees alone. He set up a network of his trainees so they could help and support one another. Cambridge Connection advisers can be found at www. CambridgeConnection.com. Whitehead, the author of *Why Smart People Do Stupid Things with Money: Overcoming Financial Dysfunction* (2009) also publishes an amusing blog about financial issues on his website.

Sheryl Garrett set up an hourly fee-only model financial planning practice in Kansas, in 1998 dedicated to serving the middle-market consumer. Working by the hour, Garrett reasoned, would better satisfy her need to make a difference with the people she most wanted to help rather than just stirring numbers around for the rich. Garrett's model is simple, good for both planner and consumer. She doesn't believe that every client needs a complete financial plan and she's willing to work piecemeal to put together what her clients need.

A couple of years later, Garrett franchised her business and it grew like wildfire. As with Kinder Life Planners, Garrett Planning Network planners are available in nearly every state. Some planners are both RLPs® and members of Garrett's network like Larry Annello in Connecticut, Helga Cuthbert in Georgia, Phil Dyer in Maryland, Michael Knight in Illinois, Derek Lenington and Madeline Moore in Oregon, Patricia Rudolph in Kentucky, and Cindy Sterling in New York.

When friends ask me to recommend an adviser, I usually suggest an RLP® or someone from the Garrett Network – at www.garrettplanning.com. I've followed up with the people I've referred to Garrett's planners and they have never been disappointed. Many of the planners will work by phone and internet if they are not close to your location.

In summary both Garrett and Cambridge Connection are fiduciaries. Most are CFPs®. Many are NAPFA members. Cambridge and Garrett put the lie to another common fallacy, which is that the only advisers middle-income clients can afford are commission-based. Given all the risks we've identified in that model, why would you want to subject the working and middle-classes to sales rather than advice, as if the only people with goals worth pursuing were people with lots of money?

The FPA, with its database of 23,000 will also have many additional advisers who are fee-only, but they may be harder for you to find. Nearly all of their advisers, however, are CFPs®, fee-transparent and fiduciaries.

In the UK

The Institute of Financial Planning (IFP) (www.financialplanning.org.uk/) is the membership organization for Certified Financial Planners®. It has a significant number of advisers who charge on a fee-only basis, but you have to search for them.

The Personal Finance Society (PFS) (www.thepfs.org/) has a smaller percentage of advisers who charge fee-only, but has a database of 20,000 advisers to choose from. Over 2000 members are Chartered Financial Planners.

Most advisers in the RLP® community (www.kinderinstitute.com) work on a fee-only or fee-transparent basis. There are quite a few who work with middle-income clients as well.

Across the globe

While financial advice is still dominated by product companies, there is a movement driven by consumers, advisers and regulators all across the world toward fees, fee-transparency and fee-only. It is particularly noticeable in Australia, the Netherlands, India, the US and the UK.

Professional Designations

Certified Financial Planners®: What the Designation Means For You

Like most professions, financial advisers carry an alphabet soup of certifications, some very important and others almost meaningless. We live in a world of specialists. We'll hire a CPA to do our taxes, an estate planning attorney to do our will, a retirement specialist to evaluate our pension or social security options, an RIA to invest with, an insurance agent to source risk products. In such a world who is it that coordinates all of these products and processes? We do, the one completely untrained person in the group. We are the ones then tasked with the most complex responsibility of all, making sure the whole package of products and services works together in our best interest, without one product undermining another, or worse yet, undermining our life ambitions without anyone seeing it. The Certified Financial Planner® designation arose from a group of visionary financial advisers who recognized that financial advice at its best and most humane would be holistic, concerned with a client's overall financial welfare and dedicated to people rather than products.

Even today, anyone can use the designation "financial planner," or "financial adviser" without any education, training or experience. This reality became a big issue for professional advisers in the 1960's, who were working to elevate the profession by devising a designation and set of standards and ethics that did mean something. They formed an organization that eventually became the Financial Planning Association

(FPA), the current champion of the Certified Financial Planner® designation. The designation is controlled by the CFP® Board of Standards, which enforced the standards and policies of the profession.

Today, the profession is regulated internationally. As of April 2010, board members and associate members come from 23 countries around the world. The board has nearly 140,000 members using the CFP® designation, 64,000 of them in the US. The CFP® mark is recognized around the world as the top credential in the planning profession. The primary objective of the CFP® Board is to "benefit the consumer public by promoting the value of professional, competent and ethical planning service by those who have earned the CFP® certification," according to CFP.net, the group's website.

CFPs® have a breadth of knowledge about money matters. Their education, which can take several years to accomplish, covers investments, risk and insurance, taxes, estate planning, retirement and general financial planning including budgets and cash flow. Indeed, as Harold Evensky, an adviser in Florida, says: "If a planner doesn't have a CFP®, move on. Period." Evensky, often called the dean of financial planning and one of the early fee-only practitioners, added: "There is no reason for a committed planner to avoid getting the CFP®."

Additional Designations

The **Chartered Financial Analyst (CFA)** is a designation awarded by the Association for Investment Management and Research in Charlottesville, Virginia, to analysts who have completed a rigorous three-year program focusing on investment analysis. A deservedly respected designation. It does not cover financial planning, other than the investments.

Certified Public Accountant (CPA) is a designation regulated by the board of accountancy in each state. CPAs must pass what is considered a difficult exam. But a CPA designation by itself is not adequate for a financial adviser. A CPA should also have either the CFP® designation or the designation for CPAs who train to become financial planners: **Personal Financial Specialist (PFS)**.

A **Chartered Life Underwriter (CLU)** is an insurance specialist trained by the American College in Bryn Mawr, PA. A CLU must have experience in the field of insurance and have completed eight college-level insurance courses. Many fine planners are CLUs. But that mark alone does not qualify someone to be an expert in financial planning. It qualifies them to sell insurance. Many a financial planner has started as a CLU and then become a CFP® as well.

The American College also issues the designation of **Chartered Financial Consultant (ChFC)** to insurance agents who take a total of nine college courses. This, too, is an insurance designation.

The **National Association of Personal Financial Advisers (NAPFA)**, founded in 1983, has 2400 members who pride themselves on three things: They are fiduciaries, which means they put the client's need first rather than an employer's. They are compensated strictly by fees paid by the consumer. That frees them from a conflict of interest over how much compensation they might receive from various vendors. They believe in holistic financial planning, looking at the entire individual rather than just a segment such as insurance or retirement planning. Most are CFPs®.

A **Registered Investment Adviser (RIA)** is an individual or firm that has filed with the Securities and Exchange Commission. The RIA designation does not mean that the firm or individual is approved in any way by the SEC. But it does show that the adviser is in compliance with the registration requirement and is a fiduciary.

A **Registered Life Planner® (RLP®)** has been trained by the Kinder Institute of Life Planning to do extensive work with a client exploring his life goals and dreams and helping him find a way to achieve them. This Life Planning work precedes the traditional financial side of planning such as risk management, investing, estate planning, etc. An RLP® has spent at least 100 hours in training sessions, seminars and working with a mentor to discover how to best develop a total Life Plan for a client. Most are CFPs® as well, and/or Chartered in the UK.

A **Registered Representative** is a stockbroker who has passed a series of securities exams and is registered with a broker/dealer and regulated by the National Association of Securities Dealers. Registered

Representatives need not – and often do not – do financial planning. Many financial advisers argue that a registered rep is simply a securities salesman, as compared to a financial planner who looks at all of a client's needs. Not a fiduciary.

Additional UK designation

A **Chartered Financial Planner** receives their designation from the Chartered Insurance Institute. Although Certified is the international standard, Chartered is the strongest and most dynamic brand in the UK right now, growing rapidly with the professional designation requirements of the RDR regulations. Generally considered the equivalent to certified status, the examinations leading to the Chartered designation have a more technical focus than the planning focused CFP® exam. Many of the top Independent Financial Advisers (IFAs) in the UK hold both designations.

Additional European designation

In Europe, look for the CFP®, but where it is not available, the closest designation is the European Financial Planner designation conferred by the European Financial Planning Association.

Global

To search for one of the 75,000 CFPs® practicing outside the US visit the Financial Planning Standards Board website, www.FPSB.org. There you will find both databases of country-by-country associations of financial planners as well as individual practitioners.

The Great Firm of the Future

If the great financial advisory firm of the future, the new branded financial services firm were to suddenly appear, how would you recognize it? What would the buzz be? What would it deliver?

1. First of all, the entire firm would have a reputation for the highest standards of integrity, fiduciary standards, and would be respected for these standards at all levels of the firm – by its employees, by consumers, by the media and by the financial profession.

2. Second, the buzz would be that the firm delivers the freedom to clients they long to have to live their ideal lives. Everyone in the firm would be known for their great listening skills, their care, their empathy and their capacity to inspire – their ability to see what is special in each of us, and to celebrate and help deliver it. It would be both a place and an experience that makes clients happy. They would be delighted to revisit again and again.

3. Third, there would be no ties of the adviser or the firm to the big financial product companies, no conflicts of interest at all with these companies. The adviser would work only for you. The firms would be fee-only, with even the smallest of potential conflicts fully disclosed and transparent. Advice would be available to people in all economic circumstances, and of all backgrounds.

4. Fourth, the standard for advice would be comprehensive financial planning and advisers would hold the professional designations required to touch on all the clients' areas of financial concern.

5. Fifth, a breath of fresh air around investment advice. Investment advice would no longer be about selling products, gambling for the best return. In fact there would be no products too complex for the client to understand nor for the adviser to explain. Clients would understand the relationship of risk to rate of return and how they are used in a systematic, simple and low cost process of investing. The goal of investing would be to deliver with greatest efficiency what's most important to the client, their Life Plan, their life of choice.

In my view delivering this kind of service establishes the financial advisory profession as among the greatest professions there have ever been, one that models integrity and delivers freedom into people's lives.

In Summary: Finding a Financial Adviser You Can Trust

It's time to do the search for the financial adviser you can trust. We've elaborated on the major criteria throughout this addendum.

Below are the various qualities we recommend in a financial adviser. Start your search by ranking all the categories in order of importance to you from 1 (least important) to 10 (extremely important). When I do this, for instance, everything is a 10 except for local which gets a 5, passive which gets an 8 and illiquid investments which gets a 2.

1. Are you local?

2. Are you an RLP®?

3. Are you a CFP®?

4. Are you fee-only?

5. Are you a fiduciary?

6. Are you passive?

7. Do you have a succession plan?

8. Do you invest for your clients in illiquid investments such as hedge funds, private equity or limited partnerships?

If you have a bunch of 10s as I do, rank them in degree of importance. When I do that, I rank RLP® and fee-only first because they are the rarest and have the smallest available databases. So I will search the database for RLPs® first, www.kinderinstitute.com, and see if I can find someone in the database who matches all my criteria, or most of my criteria. Since locality is not so important to me, I would choose advisers first who match all the other criteria that are critical for me and who are as close to where I live as possible. Once I have a few advisers I would carefully check their websites, call to talk with them, and then interview my first choices. Once there I would ask about their initial and ongoing process of client service, and I would ask for a sample of their output.

****

As we've said many times, there are terrific advisers to choose from now in the world, advisers of great integrity dedicated to your personal journey and that of your family.

I know I speak for every Life Planner when I say how excited I am at the thought of the great and meaningful adventure you are launching into as you undertake your own Life Plan. Whether or not you invite an experienced guide to go with you on the journey from the start, you now know how to find a great adviser who would consider it an honor to work with you to achieve the life you dream of living!

Books to Further Your Investment Knowledge

- *The 7 Secrets of Money: The Insider's Guide to Personal Investment Success* by Bruce Wilson, Richard Stott, Ben Sherwood and Simon Brown, Kindle Edition – 2011; Amazon UK link: http://tinyurl.com/8qovkw4

- *Winning the Loser's Game, Fifth Edition: Timeless Strategies for Successful Investing* by Charles Ellis, McGraw-Hill, 2009

- *The Intelligent Investor: The Definitive Book on Value Investing. A Book of Practical Counsel* by Benjamin Graham, Jason Zweig and Warren E. Buffett, Collins Business, 2003

- *The Little Book of Common Sense Investing: The Only Way to Guarantee Your Fair Share of Stock Market Returns (Little Books. Big Profits)* by John C. Bogle, Wiley, 2007

- *All About Asset Allocation* by Richard Ferri, McGraw-Hill, 2010

- *The Power of Passive Investing: More Wealth with Less Work* by Richard Ferri, Wiley, 2010

- *Monkey with a Pin: Why You May be Missing 6% a Year from Your Investment Returns* by Pete Comley; Amazon UK: http://tinyurl.com/8vkchn2; download for free: http://monkeywithapin.com

- *Smarter Investing – Simpler Decisions for Better Results* by Tim Hale, Financial Times/Prentice Hall, 2006; Amazon UK link: http://www.amazon.co.uk/Smarter-Investing-Simpler-Decisions-Results/dp/0273722077

- *A Random Walk Down Wall Street: The Time-Tested Strategy for Successful Investing* by Burton Malkiel, W.W. Norton & Co., 2012

Additional Books by George Kinder

- *The Seven Stages of Money Maturity – Understanding the Spirit and Value of Money in Your Life* by George Kinder, Random House, 1999

- *Lighting the Torch – The Kinder Method of Life Planning* (for Advisers) by George Kinder and Susan Galvan, FPA Press, 2006

- *Transforming Suffering into Wisdom – The Art of Inner Listening* by George Kinder, Serenity Point Press, 2010

- *A Song for Hana & the Spirit of Leho'ula* (the heart of George's Life Plan) by George Kinder, Serenity Point Press, 2007

Additional Books Cited in Text

- *Whole Child, Whole Parent* by Polly Berrien Berrends, Harper Paperbacks, 1997

- *The Number: A Completely Different Way to Think About the Rest of Your Life* by Lee Eisenberg, Free Press, 2006

- *Invest in Yourself: Six Secrets to a Rich Life* by Marc Eisenson , Gerri Detweiler and Nancy Castleman, Wiley, 2001

- *Your Money or Your Life: 9 Steps to Transforming Your Relationship with Money and Achieving Financial Independence* by Vicki Robin, Joe Dominguez and Monique Tilford, Penguin Books, 2008

- *How a Second Grader Beats Wall Street: Golden Rules Any Investor Can Learn* by Allan Roth, Wiley, 2011

- *Sheconomics* by Karen Pine and Simonne Gnessen, Headling Book Publishing, 2009

- *Changing for Good: A Revolutionary Six-Stage Program for Overcoming Bad Habits and Moving Your Life Positively Forward* by James O. Prochaska, John Norcross and Carlo DiClemente, William Morrow Paperback, 2007

27431628R00134

Made in the USA
San Bernardino, CA
13 December 2015